A RECOVERING RED

STEPS

GOSPEL-CENTERED RECOVERY

Member Book

MATT CHANDLER
MICHAEL SNETZER

LifeWay Press®
Nashville, Tennessee

Published by LifeWay Press® • © 2015 The Village Church

No part of this book may be reproduced or transmitted in any form or by any means, electronic or mechanical, including photocopying and recording, or by any information storage or retrieval system, except as may be expressly permitted in writing by the publisher. Requests for permission should be addressed in writing to LifeWay Press®; One LifeWay Plaza; Nashville, TN 37234-0152.

ISBN 978-1-4300-3214-4 • Item 005644097
Dewey decimal classification: 248.84 • Subject headings: DISCIPLESHIP / CHRISTIAN LIFE / SIN

Scripture quotations are taken from The Holy Bible, English Standard Version® (ESV®), copyright © 2001 by Crossway, a publishing ministry of Good News Publishers. Used by permission. All rights reserved.

To order additional copies of this resource, write to LifeWay Resources Customer Service; One LifeWay Plaza; Nashville, TN 37234-0113; fax 615.251.5933; phone toll free 800.458.2772; order online at *www.lifeway.com;* email *orderentry@lifeway.com;* or visit the LifeWay Christian Store serving you.

Printed in the United States of America

Groups Ministry Publishing • LifeWay Resources • One LifeWay Plaza • Nashville, TN 37234-0152

Contents

Introduction to *Steps* Discipleship

> Jesus came and said to them, "All authority in heaven and on earth
> has been given to me. Go therefore and make disciples of all nations,
> baptizing them in the name of the Father and of the Son and of the
> Holy Spirit, teaching them to observe all that I have commanded you.
> And behold, I am with you always, to the end of the age."
> **MATTHEW 28:18-20**

The mission of *Steps* fits into the church's greater mission of bringing glory to God by making disciples through gospel-centered worship, gospel-centered community, gospel-centered service, and gospel-centered multiplication. *Steps* is an intensive discipleship program that consists of daily Bible study and reflection, one-on-one mentoring, sharing in small groups, and a large-group teaching time.

FIVE PARTS OF STEPS

1. SMALL GROUPS
BIBLICAL COMMUNITY
Relationships are necessary components to our spiritual growth. We recommend that each person entering *Steps* be in biblical community. During the first hour of each week's group session, participants are divided into small groups by gender. These small groups range in size but ideally have no more than 12 participants. The group leader begins with prayer and then guides discussion. We encourage relationships begun in the groups to grow outside the groups. This happens when participants get together outside their small groups to encourage one another and to grow into deeper relationships.

2. TEACHING
SITTING UNDER THE WORD
The other hour is spent in the large group with a related video teaching for the week's study.

3. MENTORS
PERSONAL DISCIPLESHIP
Mentors are believers who have faithfully completed the *Steps* program and the necessary training and have developed sufficient spiritual maturity to disciple someone else. Participants and mentors are responsible to meet together weekly.

It is one thing to guide someone through a program; it is a much different thing to encourage others in their relationship with Christ and to teach all He has commanded His followers. It is important for a mentor to be able to do both.

4. DAILY STUDY
FEEDING ON THE WORD
Daily homework—a combination of Bible study, reflection, and prayer—is required throughout the *Steps* program. In addition, "Going Deeper" questions are designed to challenge participants to honestly and prayerfully examine their lives in light of the Scriptures they are studying. Participants then bring these reflections to their leader and share what the Lord has revealed. This process will obviously be uncomfortable for some participants, but over time it will build intimacy within a safe environment.

5. ASSESSMENT
EQUIPPING IN CONFESSION AND REPENTANCE
In the middle of the program (weeks 5–7), we will transition from homework to assessment work. This is a time of reflecting on and writing about specific sins, situations, and relationships that may be robbing us of the freedom we have in Christ. At the end of this period, the study returns to the devotional-style homework.

We should not view *Steps* as an attempt to climb a staircase to God through a religious system but rather as a pursuit of obedience in faithful response to what God has already accomplished and promised through the gospel of Jesus Christ.

Steps begins by laying the foundation of what Jesus has accomplished on the cross for those who believe (gospel truths) and then bids people to live out the call to follow Christ (gospel pursuits). To clarify, we are not trying to legitimize the traditional 12 steps. Instead, we will examine and deconstruct each step, claim whatever truth it may hold, reconstruct the step within a biblical framework, and apply it within a gospel context.

No one can lay a foundation other than that which is laid, which is
Jesus Christ. Now if anyone builds on the foundation with gold, silver,
precious stones, wood, hay, straw—each one's work will become
manifest, for the Day will disclose it, because it will be revealed by
fire, and the fire will test what sort of work each one has done.
1 CORINTHIANS 3:11-13

For freedom Christ has set us free; stand firm therefore,
and do not submit again to a yoke of slavery.
GALATIANS 5:1

My Goal and Commitment

On the lines below, identify your hope and desire as you begin this process. What do you hope to gain from this experience? What do you hope to come away with at the end of this process? Why are you committing to the next 13 weeks of *Steps?*

_____

_____

_____

_____

_____

_____

_____

_____

_____

_____

Review the following statements. If you agree to the expectations of this process, check each box, sign your name, and date your commitment.

NOTE: *Steps* is not just a personal commitment. Your commitment is to the entire group, including the other members, your leader, and your mentor.

- ☐ I commit to complete the personal study and assessments each week during *Steps*.
- ☐ I commit to be honest with myself, my group, my leader, my mentor, and God.
- ☐ I commit to be present for the group session each week.
- ☐ I commit to participate in the discussion and to actively listen during the teaching.

_____

Signature   Date

My Group Information

DAY AND TIME   LOCATION

MY GROUP LEADER   CONTACT INFORMATION

MY MENTOR   CONTACT INFORMATION

MENTOR DAY AND TIME   LOCATION

GROUP MEMBERS   CONTACT INFORMATION

NOTES

CREATION AND FALL

Viewer Guide I

COMPLETE THIS VIEWER GUIDE AS YOU WATCH THE VIDEO FOR SESSION 1.

There is only one God, and He alone _created_ all things.

There's a response that God has to His creation: it was _good_.

God endows and bestows a _dignity_ and a _worth_ on this special part of creation known as man and woman.

In His authority God is establishing _boundaries_ and giving instructions for how humanity can flourish.

The Bible is laying forth a correct _diagnosis_ of what has gone awry in the world and in your heart and mine.

God created humanity for a purpose: to _relate_ to Him and _enjoy_ Him and _glorify_ Him forever.

You and I, since the fall, have been in a posture and a position of _rebellion_ and enmity against the true God.

What you and I have earned because of our sin, what we deserve because of sin, is _death_.

An eternal punishment is just because there's a holy and righteous God we have _offended_.

Sin is not simply _what_ you do. It's _who_ you are.

I am a child of _wrath_, and I have been since the beginning.

I need a _rescuer_!

To the beautiful, God says, "You're _broken_."

To the broken, God says He's in the business of _re-creating_.

Why Gospel-Centered Recovery?

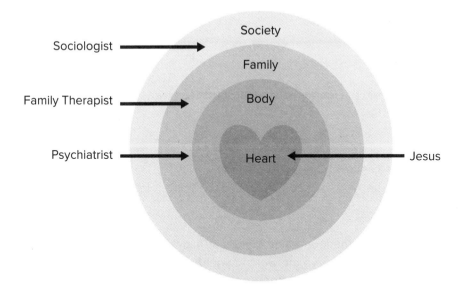

Sociologist →
Family Therapist →
Psychiatrist →

Society
Family
Body
Heart

Jesus ←

John Henderson, *Equipped to Counsel* (Bedford, TX: Association of Biblical Counselors, 2008).

NOTES

Sin is lawlessness (John)
Roman 6-23
Ephesians 2-03

DAY 1

Introducing the Creator

In the beginning God laid the foundation of the world in an awesome display of His immeasurable power:

> O LORD, our Lord,
>> how majestic is your name in all the earth!
> You have set your glory above the heavens.
> **PSALM 8:1**

> You, Lord, laid the foundation of the earth in the beginning,
>> and the heavens are the work of your hands.
> **HEBREWS 1:10**

READ GENESIS 1:1–2:3.

1. Who is the central character introduced in the creation narrative? Who is ultimately inspiring the writer to write? What does this tell us about our Creator's desire for us to know Him?

2. What characteristics of our Creator can be observed in this opening scene?

3. What was the result when God spoke? How might this affect our confidence in God to deliver on His promises or in His ability to carry them out?

> By faith we understand that the universe was created by the word of
> God, so that what is seen was not made out of things that are visible.
> **HEBREWS 11:3**

4. How did the Creator describe His creative design?

5. What rhythm and order do you see in the creation account? What verbs describe how the Creator transformed what is without form and void?

POINT OF INTEREST: God assigns a place, meaning, and value to creation. Attempting to find place, meaning, and value apart from His assignment is futile.

> Worthy are you, our Lord and God,
>   to receive glory and honor and power,
> for you created all things,
>   and by your will they existed and were created.
> **REVELATION 4:11**

6. How did God make humankind distinct from the rest of His creation?

> When I look at your heavens, the work of your fingers,
>   the moon and the stars, which you have set in place,
> what is man that you are mindful of him,
>   and the son of man that you care for him?
> Yet you have made him a little lower than the heavenly beings
>   and crowned him with glory and honor.
> You have given him dominion over the works of your hands;
>   you have put all things under his feet.
> **PSALM 8:3-6**

8. What words in Genesis 1:26 suggest a trinitarian God? Since polytheism (many gods) is inconsistent with Christianity (see Deut. 6:4), how can you explain the use of "Let us," knowing God is one (monotheism)?

> In the beginning was the Word, and the Word was with God, and the Word was God. He was in the beginning with God. All things were made through him, and without him was not anything made that was made.
> **JOHN 1:1-3**

9. What did God command Adam and Eve to do? As image bearers, how were they to steward the creation? How does naming suggest authority?

10. Genesis 1:28 says God spoke to Adam and Eve. When God spoke the rest of creation into existence, did He speak *to* it? What does this simple word *to* suggest?

11. What is the significance of God's establishing a pattern of rest on the seventh day and making it holy?

> [Jesus] said to them, "The Sabbath was made for man, not man for the Sabbath."
> **MARK 2:27**

POINT OF INTEREST: The Hebrew word for *God* is *Elohim*. It is found in Genesis 1:1 in the plural form. The word *created, bara,* is found in Genesis 1:1 in the singular form. The fact that a plural form of the noun *God* is paired with the singular form of the verb *created* is fascinating, suggesting plurality within the Godhead, who is one.

FOR FURTHER STUDY: Psalm 95:1-7a; 146:5-6; Isaiah 40:25-29; 54:5; Colossians 1:15-19

The Creation of Man

READ GENESIS 2:4-25.

1. What are some examples of God's provision in these verses?

> Abraham called the name of that place, "The LORD will provide";
> as it is said to this day, "On the mount of the LORD it shall be provided."
> **GENESIS 22:14**

2. According to Genesis 2:7, how did Adam become a living creature?

3. Who made things grow in the garden?

4. Who caused it to rain?

5. According to Genesis 2:15, what was Adam's role in the garden?

6. What command did God give to Adam when He placed him in the garden? Did He want to harm or protect him?

7. Why was it not good for Adam to be alone?

8. How did God form Eve? What role did He give her?

9. What does God's care in creation show you about His character?

10. Describe a world without shame.

11. In reflecting on the garden paradise, do you believe God is for our enjoyment and pleasure?

POINT OF INTEREST: In verse 4 a personal name is given to the Creator: Yahweh (translated *L ORD*). This covenantal name of God sets Him apart as self-sufficient, self-sustaining, and the Creator of all things.

FOR FURTHER STUDY OF YAHWEH: Exodus 3:13-15; 1 Chronicles 16:23-29; Psalm 102:27; 105:1-7; Jeremiah 16:19-21; John 8:58

Marriage: God's Idea

READ GENESIS 2:18-25.

1. According to Genesis 2:24, what actions happen when a man and a woman marry? What is the significance of the separation and union that occur in marriage?

2. Whose idea is marriage?

3. Because God instituted marriage, what does this imply about God's authority to govern marriage?

4. Whose idea is sex ("They shall become one flesh")?

5. Because God created sex, what does this imply about God's authority to govern sex?

READ MATTHEW 19:1-10.

6. When the Pharisees questioned Jesus about the lawfulness of divorce, where in Scripture did He take them? What instruction did He give them?

7. What reason did Jesus give for Moses' instruction in regulating divorce?

8. What sin did Jesus say a person commits by divorcing and marrying another?

9. What exception did He give?

POINT OF INTEREST: Pastors and theologians disagree over the exact meaning of this "exception clause" and whether it frees a husband or a wife to pursue divorce in the case of adultery. Regardless of where someone lands on this question, what is undeniably clear throughout the Scriptures is that reconciliation is the preferred and best option. Someone who is experiencing adultery, abuse, abandonment, or deep discontentment in their marriage is encouraged to engage the church to shepherd them through the hurt, pain, and next steps (see 1 Cor. 6:1-8).

10. How did Jesus' disciples respond in Matthew 19:10?

To the married I give this charge (not I, but the Lord): the
wife should not separate from her husband (but if she does,
she should remain unmarried or else be reconciled to her
husband), and the husband should not divorce his wife.

1 CORINTHIANS 7:10-11

11. What instruction did Paul give to married believers?

GLIMPSE OF THE GOSPEL: God brought forth Adam's bride from Adam's wounded side. Adam awakened in celebration to claim Eve as his own in the most intimate of all human relationships without shame. Eve foreshadows the bride of Christ, the church, which is brought forth from the wounds of Christ. He too awakened in celebration to claim the church as His own in the most intimate of all relationships without shame.

MEDITATE ON THE FOLLOWING VERSE.

A man shall leave his father and his mother and hold fast
to his wife, and they shall become one flesh.

GENESIS 2:24

The Origins of Sin and Suffering

The thief comes only to steal and kill and destroy.
I came that they may have life and have it abundantly.
JOHN 10:10

READ GENESIS 3.

1. What do we learn about the serpent in verse 1? Why might we suspect that
    this is more than a mere snake?

[The angel] seized the dragon, that ancient serpent, who is
the devil and Satan, and bound him for a thousand years.
REVELATION 20:2

2. How did the serpent twist God's words? What was his motive?

POINT OF INTEREST: The serpent avoided using God's personal and covenantal
name, Yahweh, as he encountered the woman.

3. How did the serpent initially challenge Eve about God's commands?

4. Compare and contrast the way Eve expressed God's command in Genesis 3:3
    with the command God gave Adam in Genesis 2:16-17.

5. Considering that the serpent used doubt to deceive, how important is it to rightly handle God's Word with confidence?

6. What did the serpent suggest to Eve about the character of God?

7. What reasoning did Eve use when she ate of the fruit in verse 6? What did she fail to consider?

8. Where was Adam during this exchange? Instead of following God's instruction, what did Adam do?

9. For what did Adam and Eve exchange the goodness and glory of God?

... because they exchanged the truth about God for a lie and worshiped and served the creature rather than the Creator, who is blessed forever! Amen.
ROMANS 1:25

10. As a result of Adam and Eve's disobedience, how would pain and suffering be evident in their lives?

MEDITATE ON THE FOLLOWING VERSE.

Just as sin came into the world through one man, and death through sin, and so death spread to all men because all sinned ...
ROMANS 5:12

The Remedy for Insanity

REREAD GENESIS 3:7-24.

1. According to verse 7, what did Adam and Eve realize after falling into sin? How did they initially attempt to remedy their action?

2. In verse 8 what did they hear? How did they react?

3. Who lovingly pursued Adam and Eve in their disobedience? Did He seem surprised or panicked?

4. According to verse 10, why did Adam and Eve hide from God? Did the couple's attempt to remedy the problem work? Why or why not?

5. How did Adam and Eve respond to God's questioning?

6. What hope do you see in the midst of this tragedy of sin and suffering (see v. 15)?

GLIMPSE OF THE GOSPEL: Scholars often refer to verse 15 as the *protoevangelium,* or *first gospel.* Some consider it the first prophecy of the coming Messiah, fulfilled in Jesus Christ.

7.   What meaning was behind Adam's naming his wife Eve (see v. 20)? What did God say in verse 15 that might lead Adam to give her such a name?

8.   What is the covering that God provided for Adam and Eve? Why do you think He chose this covering?

> Under the law almost everything is purified with blood, and
> without the shedding of blood there is no forgiveness of sins.
> **HEBREWS 9:22**

GLIMPSE OF THE GOSPEL: Animal skins require the shedding of blood. God's provision of covering foreshadows the Old Testament sacrificial system for the atonement of sin through the shedding of innocent blood. This, in turn, looks forward to the New Testament, where Jesus became the perfect, sinless sacrifice to take away the sins of the world.

9.   According to Genesis 3, why did God send Adam and Eve out of the garden?

10. Compare and contrast verse 24 with the following verse. What might you conclude from this analysis?

> Jesus said to him, "I am the way, and the truth, and the
> life. No one comes to the Father except through me."
> **JOHN 14:6**

Another Way?

READ GENESIS 4:1-16.

1. How did Cain respond when God rejected his offering in verse 5?

> By faith Abel offered to God a more acceptable sacrifice than Cain,
> through which he was commended as righteous, God commending him by
> accepting his gifts. And through his faith, though he died, he still speaks.
> **HEBREWS 11:4**

2. According to Hebrews 11:4, what made Abel's sacrifice acceptable?

3. Did God encourage Cain to repent? What did He say?

4. How was Cain's response when God questioned him different from Adam's response in Genesis 3:12?

> Whoever conceals his transgressions will not prosper.
> **PROVERBS 28:13**

5. What was Cain's response to the Lord's discipline in Genesis 4:13? About whom was he most concerned?

MEDITATE ON THE FOLLOWING VERSE.

For the moment all discipline seems painful rather than pleasant, but later it yields the peaceful fruit of righteousness to those who have been trained by it.
HEBREWS 12:11

Going Deeper

> Man's chief end is to glorify God, and to enjoy Him forever.
> **WESTMINSTER CATECHISM**

1. What do you think it means to fear the Lord?

> The fear of the LORD is the beginning of wisdom,
> and the knowledge of the Holy One is insight.
> **PROVERBS 9:10**

2. Where does your heart go when you read the creation account?

3. Where does your heart go when you consider the suffering, pain, and hardship of our fallen world?

4. How does understanding God's pursuit and plan for redemption affect you?

5. According to the creation account, a functional human being is to live in a loving, dependent relationship with his Creator. In what areas of your life do you rely on creation rather than the Creator for direction, protection, provision, power, satisfaction, comfort, security, stability, hope, and happiness?

> My people have committed two evils:
> they have forsaken me,
>   the fountain of living waters,
> and hewed out cisterns for themselves,
>   broken cisterns that can hold no water.
> **JEREMIAH 2:13**

6. Describe your current suffering. What is the source?

7. God created us to be in loving relationships with Himself and others. Think about your close community and friends. Do you reach out to others when you need help? Why or why not? Where do they point you for hope?

8. In what ways do you disregard God's voice and follow another voice to pursue your own desires?

9. What do you do and where do you turn in your sin and suffering?

10. How do you attempt to remedy the problem? Or are you just defeated?

I do not nullify the grace of God, for if righteousness
were through the law, then Christ died for no purpose.
GALATIANS 2:21

STEP 1: We admitted we were powerless over our addictions and compulsive behaviors—that our lives had become unmanageable.

You were dead in the trespasses and sins in which you once
walked, following the course of this world, following the prince of
the power of the air, the spirit that is now at work in the sons of
disobedience—among whom we all once lived in the passions of
our flesh, carrying out the desires of the body and the mind, and
were by nature children of wrath, like the rest of mankind.
EPHESIANS 2:1-3

Just as sin came into the world through one man, and death
through sin, and so death spread to all men because all sinned ...
ROMANS 5:12

REDEEMED TRUTH FROM STEP 1: Man, in relationship to his Creator, has fallen from a place of dignity, humility, and dependence to a state of depravity, pride, and rebellion. This has led to unfathomable suffering. Any attempts on our own to redeem ourselves are futile, only increasing the problem of independence and self-sufficiency. Any perceived success leads only to empty vanity. Apart from Christ, we are powerless to overcome sin, and our attempts to control it only increase our chaos.

THE REMEDY: THE GOSPEL

Viewer Guide 2

COMPLETE THIS VIEWER GUIDE AS YOU WATCH THE VIDEO FOR SESSION 2.

The world will come in and offer a false solution, a false hope, a false _gospel_.

Redemption: the _freedom_ purchased through a ransom, paid by a redeemer on behalf of the enslaved

There was an amount that we owed because of being enslaved to sin. Jesus, on the cross, paid the price for our freedom and _redeemed_ us.

The Enemy works through the world to entice the flesh, and it reveals that the brokenness is coming from our own _hearts_.

In the insanity of running to created things, we are looking to a physical thing to solve a _spiritual_ problem.

Whatever is in that seat of highest worship in our life, we will _pursue_ and _sacrifice_ for it.

We can just as easily trade in unrighteousness for self-righteousness when what we really need is _Christ_ righteousness.

Jesus reaches into the cycle; interrupts the cycle; and offers a real solution, the true _gospel_ solution.

The offer of redemption is to be set free, not to rule your own life but redemption by way of getting a better _Master_ —Jesus.

The Insanity Cycle of Sin

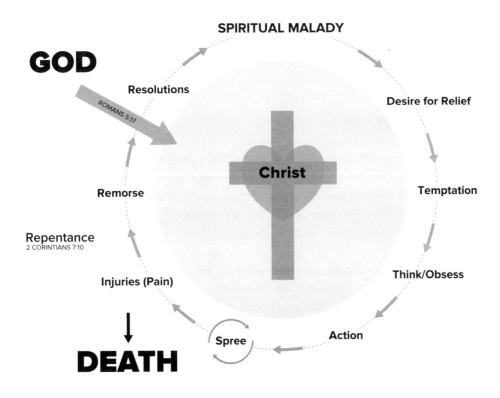

SPIRITUAL MALADY

GOD

Resolutions

ROMANS 5:17

Desire for Relief

Christ

Remorse

Temptation

Repentance
2 CORINTIANS 7:10

Injuries (Pain)

Think/Obsess

↓
DEATH

Spree

Action

NOTES

Romans 8:22-23

DAY 1

The Law

READ DEUTERONOMY 5:1-22.

These verses contain the Ten Commandments that God gives Moses at Mount Sinai. Apart from God's grace, man will attempt to deal with God's law by either rebelling against it (unrighteousness) or attempting to reconcile himself to God by his own efforts (self-righteousness). Both approaches are unrighteous, for each attempts to remedy the problem of sin independent from God.

> By works of the law no human being will be justified in his
> sight, since through the law comes knowledge of sin.
> **ROMANS 3:20**

1. According to this verse, what comes through the law? Can the law justify us in God's eyes?

READ MATTHEW 5:17-48.

2. According to verse 17, why did Christ come? What does this purpose mean for us?

3. In verse 27 Jesus quoted the law. Verse 28 reveals the spirit behind the law. What did Jesus address in the last word of verse 28?

THINK ABOUT THE FOLLOWING VERSE.

Woe to you, scribes and Pharisees, hypocrites! For you are like
whitewashed tombs, which outwardly appear beautiful, but
within are full of dead people's bones and all uncleanness.
MATTHEW 23:27

4. Based on your understanding of today's verses, who were the Pharisees?
    With what posture did they approach the law, and how did they
    misinterpret and misapply it? How did Jesus view this approach?

5. In Matthew 5:17-48 Jesus gave a more robust understanding of what truths?
    How might Jesus' explanation have destroyed any self-righteousness?

MEDITATE ON THE FOLLOWING VERSE.

God has done what the law, weakened by the flesh,
could not do. By sending his own Son in the likeness
of sinful flesh and for sin, he condemned sin in the flesh.
ROMANS 8:3

The Extent of God's Justice and Man's Sin

READ GENESIS 6:5-22.

1. According to the narrative of Noah and the flood, how far was God willing to go in order to bring judgment against sin?

2. How did God preserve Noah's life?

READ EXODUS 11:1–12:13.

3. According to this narrative, how far was God willing to go in order to bring about justice?

4. How did God preserve the Israelites' lives?

5. How does the reality of hell demonstrate the way God views the severity of sin (see Matt. 13:47-50; 25:31-46; John 3:36)?

6. What does the cross of Christ communicate about how far God was willing to go in order to wipe out evil (sin)?

> Enter by the narrow gate. For the gate is wide and the way is easy
> that leads to destruction, and those who enter by it are many.
> **MATTHEW 7:13**

READ ROMANS 1:18–2:3.

7. How does humankind "by their unrighteousness suppress the truth" (v. 18)?

8. In response to humanity's actions, how does God carry out His wrath? What does He give them over to?

9. How is unrighteousness, or sin, defined in verse 25?

10. According to verses 29-32, with what are we filled?

11. Romans 2:1-3 addresses the self-righteous. How does God respond to the attitude "Thank You that I am not like them" (see Luke 18:9-14)?

MEDITATE ON THE FOLLOWING VERSES.

Regarding the extent of sin:

All have sinned and fall short of the glory of God.
ROMANS 3:23

Regarding the extent of God's justice:

The wages of sin is death, but the free gift of God
is eternal life in Christ Jesus our Lord.
ROMANS 6:23

POINT OF INTEREST: The law confines a person to the pursuit of outward obedience, but it cannot address the heart. Only the gospel cures the heart of injustice.

Prophecy:
The Suffering Servant

READ ISAIAH 52:7–53:12.

This is the last of three prophetic songs in Isaiah that describe the Suffering Servant, Jesus, who would redeem the world.

1.   Read Isaiah 52:7. How is this news described?

2.   How does verse 13 describe the Suffering Servant's actions? What would be the result of those actions?

> Being found in human form, he humbled himself by becoming obedient
> to the point of death, even death on a cross. Therefore God has highly
> exalted him and bestowed on him the name that is above every name.
> **PHILIPPIANS 2:8-9**

3.   According to Isaiah 52:14, why would people be taken aback by Jesus? What would be accomplished (see v. 15)?

POINT OF INTEREST: "So shall he sprinkle many nations" (v. 15) means they will be made clean through Jesus' atoning work.

FOR FURTHER STUDY OF THE MINISTRY OF SPRINKLING: Exodus 29:21; Leviticus 4:1-21; 14:7; 16:14-19; Hebrews 9:13-14,19-22; 10:19-22; 12:22-24; 1 Peter 1:2.

4. Why might it have been difficult to put your hope in Christ based on appearance alone (see Isa. 53:2)?

> We preach Christ crucified, a stumbling block to Jews and folly to Gentiles, but to those who are called, both Jews and Greeks, Christ the power of God and the wisdom of God. For the foolishness of God is wiser than men, and the weakness of God is stronger than men.
> **1 CORINTHIANS 1:23-25**

5. What was it like to be in Jesus' shoes (see Isa. 53:3)?

6. Why was Jesus wounded and crushed?

> He shall bruise your head,
> and you shall bruise his heel.
> **GENESIS 3:15**

7. How did Jesus respond to those who hated Him?

> When he was reviled, he did not revile in return; when he suffered, he did
> not threaten, but continued entrusting himself to him who judges justly.
> **1 PETER 2:23**

8. Though He was crucified between two criminals and buried in a rich man's
    tomb, what was true about Jesus, according to Isaiah 53:9?

> Two robbers were crucified with him, one on the right and one on the left.
> **MATTHEW 27:38**

> When it was evening, there came a rich man from Arimathea, named
> Joseph, who also was a disciple of Jesus. He went to Pilate and asked
> for the body of Jesus. Then Pilate ordered it to be given to him. And
> Joseph took the body and wrapped it in a clean linen shroud and
> laid it in his own new tomb, which he had cut in the rock. And he
> rolled a great stone to the entrance of the tomb and went away.
> **MATTHEW 27:57-60**

9. What was God's will for the Suffering Servant (see v. 10)?

10. After God's will was fulfilled, what would the Servant see (see Isa. 53:10)?

> I will put enmity between you and the woman,
>   and between your offspring and her offspring;
> he shall bruise your head,
>   and you shall bruise his heel.
>
> **GENESIS 3:15**

11. How would victory and prolonged days (see Isa. 53:10) be possible if the Servant was to be killed?

12. Who would be satisfied? What would be satisfied (see v. 11)?

> Since, therefore, we have now been justified by his blood,
> much more shall we be saved by him from the wrath of God.
>
> **ROMANS 5:9**

POINT OF INTEREST: Isaiah wrote this prophecy approximately seven hundred years before the Suffering Servant entered the world.

13. According to chapter 54, what hope might the good news of the gospel bring to people who are suffering, specifically those struggling with infertility or the loss of a spouse?

> Father of the fatherless and protector of widows
>   is God in his holy habitation.
> God settles the solitary in a home;
>   he leads out the prisoners to prosperity,
>   but the rebellious dwell in a parched land.
> **PSALM 68:5-6**

14. In light of the hope that the good news of Isaiah 54 brings, what is the invitation in chapter 55?

DAY 4

Hope: Light Comes into the World

READ JOHN 1:1-14.

Light came into the world and rescued us from Satan, sin, shame, death, and darkness.

1. In what ways does this text sound familiar (see Gen. 1)?

2. Who is the Word (see John 1:1,14)?

3. Where was the Word during creation (see v. 2)?

4. What was done through Him (see v. 3)?

5. What is in Him (see v. 4)?

Jesus said to him, "I am the way, and the truth, and the
life. No one comes to the Father except through me."
JOHN 14:6

6. What is the life (see John 1:4)?

7. Where can we find hope in our darkness?

8. To whom does the true Light give the right to become children of God
(see v. 12)?

9. On what basis does the true Light give the right to become children of God
(see v. 13)?

MEDITATE ON THE FOLLOWING VERSE.

The wind blows where it wishes, and you hear its sound,
but you do not know where it comes from or where it
goes. So it is with everyone who is born of the Spirit.
JOHN 3:8

DAY 5

Mercy Triumphs over Judgment

READ JOHN 8:3-12.

1. Who was brought to Jesus?

2. How must she have felt?

3. According to the law, what penalty did she face?

4. How did Jesus disqualify those who may have been tempted to bring judgment against her?

5. How was Jesus uniquely qualified to bring judgment or extend mercy?

He says to Moses, "I will have mercy on whom I have mercy,
and I will have compassion on whom I have compassion."
ROMANS 9:15

6. What did Jesus do in response to the scribes and the Pharisees?

7. In extending mercy, what did Jesus call the woman to?

8. In verse 12 who did Jesus claim to be?

9. How does the account of the woman caught in adultery point to the truth of Jesus' claim?

10. Who will have the light of life?

MEDITATE ON THE FOLLOWING VERSE.

God did not send his Son into the world to condemn the world,
but in order that the world might be saved through him.
JOHN 3:17

To an Unknown God

READ ACTS 17:16-34.

1. In verse 16 why was Paul's spirit provoked?

2. What did Paul begin to preach in the synagogue and marketplace?

3. How did some of the philosophers characterize Paul and his preaching?

4. How did they respond to Paul?

> ... always learning and never able to arrive at a knowledge of the truth.
> **2 TIMOTHY 3:7**

5. How did Paul use his knowledge of the Athenian culture to present the gospel?

6. In verse 28 Paul engaged the culture by quoting their own poets. Rather than debating them, he said in verse 29 that if what they were saying was true, what else must be true? What should not be worshiped?

7. Is it wise to form your own conception of God?

> While Paul was waiting for them at Athens, his spirit was
> provoked within him as he saw that the city was full of idols.
> **ACTS 17:16**

8. Based on the Athenians' idolatry and vain religion, what does God command all people to do (see v. 30)? Why?

9. In what three ways did Paul's audience respond?

Going Deeper

1. In what ways do you suppress the truth or live in denial (see Rom. 1:18)?

2. Do you find yourself acting like a rebellious lawbreaker or a self-righteous Pharisee? How does that tendency express itself in your life?

3. If the antidote to unrighteousness is not self-righteousness, what is it?

4. What about Christ and the gospel did you find beautiful this week?

5. To what or to whom did you look for hope and love in the past? In what or in whom did you place your trust?

6. How did Paul clarify what the Athenians worshiped as "the unknown god" (Acts 17:23)? What might be the dangers of a vague spirituality?

7. Scripture is clear: we must make a decision about our belief in Jesus. What hangs in the balance if we do nothing?

> Whoever believes in him is not condemned, but whoever
> does not believe is condemned already, because he has
> not believed in the name of the only Son of God.
> **JOHN 3:18**

8. How have you responded to the invitation to trust in the Suffering Servant?

> Come to me, all who labor and are heavy laden, and I will give you rest.
> **MATTHEW 11:28**

9. If you believe in Christ, describe how you came to believe. Use a separate sheet of paper if necessary.

STEP 2: We came to believe that a power greater than ourselves could restore us to sanity.

God, being rich in mercy, because of the great love with which he
loved us, even when we were dead in our trespasses, made us alive
together with Christ—by grace you have been saved—and raised us
up with him and seated us with him in the heavenly places in Christ
Jesus, so that in the coming ages he might show the immeasurable
riches of his grace in kindness toward us in Christ Jesus. For by grace
you have been saved through faith. And this is not your own doing;
it is the gift of God, not a result of works, so that no one may boast.
EPHESIANS 2:4-9

REDEEMED TRUTH FROM STEP 2: God lovingly intervened into our chaos and provided a remedy for the insanity of sin and the way back into fellowship with Him. We believe that by grace through faith in Jesus Christ, we can be redeemed.

If, because of one man's trespass, death reigned through that one man,
much more will those who receive the abundance of grace and the free
gift of righteousness reign in life through the one man Jesus Christ.
ROMANS 5:17

THE RESPONSE: REPENTANCE

Viewer Guide 3

COMPLETE THIS VIEWER GUIDE AS YOU WATCH THE VIDEO FOR SESSION 3.

We have treated the gospel cheaply, while the gospel is actually _____. We have treated grace cheaply when grace is _____.

The gospel—the good news—is that God did not leave us in that state but rather did act, did _____. And His intervention was in His Son, Jesus Christ.

The good news is that in the offering of Jesus Christ—life that was righteous, sacrificed for our sake—we are _____ by grace through faith.

You cannot love _____ and love God.

God has commanded all of us, in light of our sin, to _____. It means literally to turn around.

Grace is not permission to run after things and not worry about ramifications or consequences, but rather, grace is a call out of those things to _____ and to _____.

Our gratitude is contingent on the _____ of the gift we've received.

We _____ against temptation in repentance.

God has not provided you as the escape. God has provided _____.

GAMES WE PLAY WHEN FACED WITH SIN
1. We _____ the sorrow.
2. We _____ it up.
3. We run to _____.
4. We make _____.

Repentance starts with understanding that God _____ and I don't, that God is _____ and I am finite.

GODLY REPENTANCE	WORLDLY SORROW
VERTICAL	HORIZONTAL
FOCUSED ON GOD & OTHERS	FOCUSED ON SELF
SPIRITUAL	EMOTIONAL
WILLING	DEMANDING
ACTIVE	PASSIVE
HOPEFUL	HOPELESS
GRATEFUL	BEGRUDGING
PERSEVERING	TEMPORARY
HUMBLE	PRIDEFUL

NOTES

_____

_____

_____

_____

_____

_____

_____

_____

_____

_____

DAY 1

Faith Is Active

READ JAMES 2:14-26.

1. What is the essential question in verse 14? What practical example is given in verses 15-16?

2. What answer is given in verse 17 about faith apart from works?

3. Why is belief not enough? What example does verse 19 provide?

4. What should saving faith produce?

5. Can works alone save you?

By grace you have been saved through faith. And this is not your own doing; it is the gift of God, not a result of works, so that no one may boast.
EPHESIANS 2:8-9

6. What two examples did James offer of faith that saves?

7. What other truth does James 2:26 compare to "faith apart from works"?

8. What do you learn from this passage about the relationship between faith and works?

POINT OF INTEREST: *Sola fide* is Latin for *by faith alone. Sola gratia* is *by grace alone. Solo Christo* is *through Christ alone.* These, along with *sola Scriptura (by Scripture alone)* and *soli Deo gloria (glory to God alone)* make up the five *solae* of the Protestant Reformation. Though works are evidence of saving faith, they have no part in saving us.

MEDITATE ON THE FOLLOWING VERSE.

Since we have been justified by faith, we have peace
with God through our Lord Jesus Christ.
ROMANS 5:1

DAY 2

Fear of the Lord

The fear of the LORD is the beginning of wisdom,
and the knowledge of the Holy One is insight.
PROVERBS 9:10

READ ISAIAH 6.

1. How does verse 1 describe the Lord?

2. What attitude did the seraphim (angels) exhibit in the Lord's presence?

3. What were the angels singing to one another? Whom were they worshiping? Define *holy*.

POINT OF INTEREST: The ESV Study Bible note on Isaiah 6:3 says "his glory" is "a technical term for God's manifest presence with his covenant people."[1]

4. Describe Isaiah's experience in the presence of the Lord.

5. What did he confess?

> The sanctuary was filled with smoke from the glory of God
> and from his power, and no one could enter the sanctuary
> until the seven plagues of the seven angels were finished.
> **REVELATION 15:8**

> Humility is to make a right estimate of oneself.[2]
> **CHARLES SPURGEON**

6. How did the Lord extend grace in response to Isaiah's humility (see v. 7)?

> The LORD passed before him and proclaimed, "The LORD, the LORD,
> a God merciful and gracious, slow to anger, and abounding in steadfast
> love and faithfulness, keeping steadfast love for thousands, forgiving
> iniquity and transgression and sin, but who will by no means clear
> the guilty, visiting the iniquity of the fathers on the children and
> the children's children, to the third and the fourth generation."
> **EXODUS 34:6-7**

7. How did Isaiah respond to God's grace? Why was he so eager?

8. What did the Lord call him to do?

9. Why did all these things take place before Isaiah was sent into service?

1. ESV Study Bible (Wheaton, IL: Crossway Bibles, 2008), 1251.
2. Charles Spurgeon, "Pride and Humility," *The Spurgeon Archive* [online, cited 24 September 2015].
    Available from the Internet: *www.spurgeon.org/sermons/0097.htm.*

DAY 3

God's Love

READ JOHN 3:16-21.

1. What did God give so that we can have eternal life (see v. 16)? What was the cost of that gift?

2. What in God's nature and character motivated Him to give us this gift?

3. What would have happened without Jesus' coming?

4. For what purpose was Jesus sent into the world (see v. 17)?

> Everyone who believes that Jesus is the Christ has been born of God,
> and everyone who loves the Father loves whoever has been born of him.
> **1 JOHN 5:1**

5. According to John 3:18, what is true about those who believe in Christ?

POINT OF INTEREST: The original Greek language in 1 John 5:1 suggests that true belief in Jesus Christ results from being born of God. Without spiritual rebirth a person cannot truly believe. In this verse "believes" is present tense, and "has been born" is perfect tense. The use of the perfect tense suggests that the action in the past ("has been born") affects the present ("believes"). Being born of God is the foundation and cause of believing in Christ. Believing is the effect or result of being born of God. Someone does not believe unless he or she has been born again.

6.   According to verses 19-20, how do unbelievers continue to live?

7.   How do believers respond to the Light?

MEDITATE ON THE FOLLOWING VERSE.

In this the love of God was made manifest among us, that God sent
his only Son into the world, so that we might live through him.
1 JOHN 4:9

Repentance

"Yet even now," declares the LORD,
   "return to me with all your heart,
with fasting, with weeping, and with mourning;
   and rend your hearts and not your garments."
Return to the LORD your God,
   for he is gracious and merciful,
slow to anger, and abounding in steadfast love;
   and he relents over disaster.

JOEL 2:12-13

READ LUKE 15.

1. Who had gathered to hear Jesus?

2. What occurred following repentance in each of the parables?

3. Focus on the parable of the prodigal son. What is significant about the younger son's conversation with his father?

4. What did the younger son do with his inheritance?

5. Where did his choices lead him (see vv. 14-16)?

> Their end is destruction, their god is their belly, and they
> glory in their shame, with minds set on earthly things.
> **PHILIPPIANS 3:19**

6. What do you think the phrase "he came to himself" (Luke 15:17) means?

7. How was the younger son different after that?

8. How did his father receive him?

9. What did he receive from his father?

POINT OF INTEREST: The robe the father gave his son provided a covering for his filth and shame. The ring signified that he belonged to his family. His shoes symbolized that he was a son, not a slave.

10. The older brother represents the self-righteous—those who believe they "need no repentance" (v. 7). Where was the older brother during the celebration? How did the father respond to his older son's anger?

GLIMPSE OF THE GOSPEL: In reading the parable of the prodigal son, we sometimes overlook the cost of the celebration—the life of the fattened calf (see v. 23). The shed blood of an innocent calf reminds us that our reconciliation with God comes at a price: the precious, innocent Lamb of God. This fattened calf symbolizes the sufficiency of Christ as the atonement for the sins of many. The older son (the self-righteous) did not seem to value the prized calf in the same way the younger son could but spoke of it without regard for the treasure it was: "you never gave me a young goat" (v. 29). His disdain mirrors the rejection Jesus, the precious Lamb of God, experienced on earth.

MEDITATE ON THE FOLLOWING VERSE.

Godly grief produces a repentance that leads to salvation
without regret, whereas worldly grief produces death.
2 CORINTHIANS 7:10

DAY 5

Jesus Promises the Holy Spirit

> I will sprinkle clean water on you, and you shall be clean from
> all your uncleannesses, and from all your idols I will cleanse you.
> And I will give you a new heart, and a new spirit I will put within
> you. And I will remove the heart of stone from your flesh and give
> you a heart of flesh. And I will put my Spirit within you, and cause
> you to walk in my statutes and be careful to obey my rules.
> **EZEKIEL 36:25-27**

READ JOHN 14:15-31.

1. What is the evidence of our love for Christ (see v. 15)?

2. If we are powerless to do keep Jesus' commandments apart from Him, how does God help us do these things (see v. 16)?

3. How will Christ make Himself obvious to those who love Him but not to the world? (see v. 17)

4. Where does this Spirit dwell, and what does He allow us to know?

5. What does God promise His disciples (see v. 18)?

6. What does the Spirit bring (see v. 19)?

> We have received not the spirit of the world, but the Spirit who is from God, that we might understand the things freely given us by God. And we impart this in words not taught by human wisdom but taught by the Spirit, interpreting spiritual truths to those who are spiritual.
> **1 CORINTHIANS 2:12-13**

7. Christ acknowledged these things while He was still with His disciples. Whom did He identify as the Helper who would make them alive in Christ (see John 14:26)?

8. What future event did Christ refer to in verses 27-31? Who commanded this to happen?

MEDITATE ON THE FOLLOWING VERSE.

> Peter said to them, "Repent and be baptized every one of you in the name of Jesus Christ for the forgiveness of your sins, and you will receive the gift of the Holy Spirit."
> **ACTS 2:38**

DAY 6

A New Covenant

Behold, the days are coming, declares the LORD, when I will make
a new covenant with the house of Israel and the house of Judah, not
like the covenant that I made with their fathers on the day when I took
them by the hand to bring them out of the land of Egypt, my covenant
that they broke, though I was their husband, declares the LORD. For
this is the covenant that I will make with the house of Israel after those
days, declares the LORD: I will put my law within them, and I will write
it on their hearts. And I will be their God, and they shall be my people.

JEREMIAH 31:31-33

READ 2 CORINTHIANS 3:1–4:6.

1. What is the "letter from Christ" in 2 Corinthians 3:3? Who wrote it?
    Where and on what did they write it?

2. Where do we gain our confidence, competency, sufficiency, and boldness?

3. God makes us competent to be ministers of what?

65

4. Compare and contrast the ways Paul described the old and new covenants.

5. According to verse 14, who is the only One who can bring us out from under the old covenant?

6. What remains over the hearts of those who are under the old covenant?

7. What is true about those who behold the Lord with unveiled faces?

8. Having received this ministry, what do we not do (see 2 Cor. 4:1)? What do we do (see v. 2:)?

9. What is true about those to whom the gospel is veiled?

10. If God can shine light out of darkness, what hope does this truth bring to His ability to illuminate the gospel to unbelieving hearts?

11. According to verse 5, what do we proclaim?

In the same way also he took the cup, after supper, saying, "This cup is the new covenant in my blood. Do this, as often as you drink it, in remembrance of me."
1 CORINTHIANS 11:25

Going Deeper

1. If you have received the gift of faith, how has that led to a heartfelt desire to obey God?

2. Describe any experiences in which God's presence and power humbled you.

3. Describe ways the reality of God's love has affected your life.

4. Describe how you view God. What do you believe about His character, attributes, attitudes, and motivations?

5. What is your attitude toward God?

6. What is your view of humankind?

7. Define *repentance*. What has been your response to the call to repent? Why?

8. What evidence of spiritual rebirth do you see in your life?

9. Have you surrendered your life to Christ? If so, describe the process.
   If not, why?

> He died for all, that those who live might no longer live for
> themselves but for him who for their sake died and was raised.
> **2 CORINTHIANS 5:15**

STEP 3: We made a decision to turn our will and our lives over to the care of God, as you understand him.

> I appeal to you therefore, brothers, by the mercies of
> God, to present your bodies as a living sacrifice, holy and
> acceptable to God, which is your spiritual worship.
> **ROMANS 12:1**

REDEEMED TRUTH FROM STEP 3: Through the Holy Spirit's illumination of our desperate and helpless condition before God and from the hope that comes through the gospel of Jesus Christ, we step out in faith and repent as an act of worship and obedience, surrendering our will and entrusting our lives to Christ's care and control. We are reborn spiritually and rescued from the domain of darkness and brought into the kingdom of light, where we now live as a part of Christ's ever-advancing kingdom.

NOTES

THE RESULT: JUSTIFICATION, ADOPTION, AND SANCTIFICATION

Viewer Guide 4

COMPLETE THIS VIEWER GUIDE AS YOU WATCH THE VIDEO FOR SESSION 4.

What makes you a member of the kingdom of God is not the right things you do but the _____ you receive.

Rebirth or regeneration: the Spirit's work of making us _____

Conversion: the act of the regenerated person to _____, to _____, to _____, to place _____ in the work and the power of God

Justification: declaring _____

Adoption: God declares us to be _____ and _____.

Sanctification: The Holy Spirit is empowering us, but we are _____ in God's work to mature and to grow and to sanctify us.

It's your _____ that must be affected and changed for your joy. It's your heart that must _____ to fight those sin issues.

The Spirit of God is regenerating, is repairing, is fixing the _____ of our hearts.

Glorification: We are already forgiven and already accepted and already declared innocent. There is this _____ _____ of that fully being realized.

We have to know that under the covering of His grace, we can pursue honesty and transparency and openness about the ways we've _____ against God and others.

Those that are reborn into the kingdom of God cannot be _____.

This process of sanctification can be _____.

Sanctification is not all _____.

What He's providing in His Spirit is exactly what we _____ to navigate this sanctification process.

Salvation

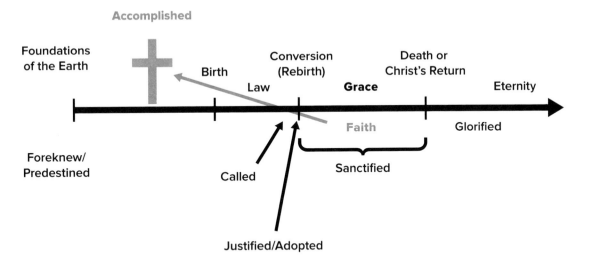

A Biblical Anthropology of the Active and the Passive Heart

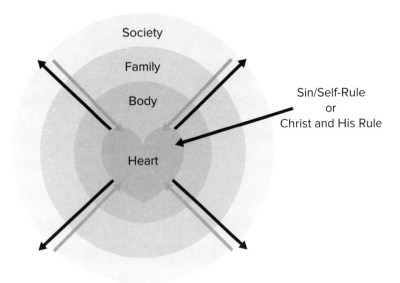

John Henderson, *Equipped to Counsel* (Bedford, TX: Association of Biblical Counselors, 2008).

DAY 1

Gospel Truths

READ ROMANS 8.

1. What is true about those who are in Christ (see v. 1)? Why? (see v. 2)? How (see vv. 3-4)?

2. How is this truth evident in the lives of those in Christ?

3. Where do those in Christ set their minds? What does this action lead to?

POINT OF INTEREST: Sanctification has two parts: mortification and vivification. Mortification is putting to death the things that rob us of our affection for Christ. Vivification is filling ourselves with the things that stir our affection for Him.

4. How do we know whether these precious truths apply to us? To whom do we belong?

5. If you live by the Spirit, what will you do, and what will be the result?

6. What does that truth reveal about our identity (see v. 14)?

POINT OF INTEREST: Adoption is an act of God that brings us into His family.

7. How is this adoption confirmed by the Spirit?

8. What does it mean to be an heir of God?

9. What future hope do we have while suffering? How are we to wait?

10. What help do we have in our suffering?

11. What is true about those who love God and are called according to His purpose?

12. What can separate us from the love of Christ (see vv. 38-39)?

DAY 2

Triumph of Grace

READ ROMANS 6.

1. Opponents of the gospel of grace (see Rom. 5) wrongly believed that grace led people to continue in sin. How did Paul respond?

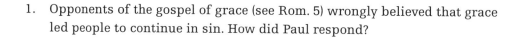

POINT OF INTEREST: *Regeneration*, according to Wayne Grudem's *Systematic Theology*, is "a secret act of God in which he imparts new spiritual life to us."[1]

2. What is certain if we have been united with Christ in death?

3. Having been crucified with Christ, what can we expect will happen to "the body of sin" (Rom. 6:6)? Why?

4. If we have died with Christ, what do we also believe (see v. 8)?

5. What did Christ accomplish when He rose from the dead (see v. 9)?

6. What does this truth mean for us?

7. What instruction does verse 12 give us?

8. How do we keep sin from reigning (see v. 13)?

9. What promise do we find in verse 14?

10. Why might someone under the old covenant, who rightly sees the law as something that restrains people, have difficulty with the gospel of grace that releases people from being under the law?

11. How did Paul counter that argument? What is now true of those under grace (see vv. 18-19)?

12. Why is obedience under grace superior to obedience under the law?

13. What is now the goal in verse 19?

MEDITATE ON THE FOLLOWING VERSE.

I am speaking in human terms, because of your natural limitations.
For just as you once presented your members as slaves to impurity
and to lawlessness leading to more lawlessness, so now present
your members as slaves to righteousness leading to sanctification.
ROMANS 6:19

1. Wayne Grudem, *Systematic Theology* (Grand Rapids, MI: Zondervan, 1994), 699.

DAY 3

A New Heart

READ MATTHEW 15:1-20.

1. The scribes and Pharisees imposed rules beyond Scripture on others and said people who did not uphold them were committing sins. What tradition did they condemn Jesus and His disciples for in verse 2?

2. How did Jesus point out the hypocrisy of the scribes and Pharisees (see vv. 3-6)?

3. How did Isaiah define a hypocrite (see vv. 8-9)?

4. What does God want more than shallow obedience?

5. Jesus used a similar example in verses 11 and 17. What did He say?

6. What defiles a person (see vv. 19-20)? Where do these things come from?

> I will sprinkle clean water on you, and you shall be clean from all your uncleannesses, and from all your idols I will cleanse you. And I will give you a new heart, and a new spirit I will put within you. And I will remove the heart of stone from your flesh and give you a heart of flesh. And I will put my Spirit within you, and cause you to walk in my statutes and be careful to obey my rules.
> **EZEKIEL 36:25-27**

DAY 4

The New Heaven and the New Earth

READ REVELATION 21–22.

1. What did John see and hear in Revelation 21:1-4?

2. What did the person sitting on the throne say in verse 5?

3. Who is this person, as identified in verse 6?

4. What promises did He give in verses 6-7?

5. What warning is given to those who reject the gift of life and cling to their former identities?

6. Summarize the description of the New Jerusalem.

7. What stands out most in Revelation 22:6-21 about Jesus' return?

READ 1 PETER 1:3-9.

8. According to verse 3, to what have we been born again? Through what?

9. Describe the inheritance mentioned in verse 4. What do these words mean? Through whom is the inheritance kept?

10. What allows us to rejoice during times of grief and difficulty?

11. What is the evidence that these promises are yours by faith?

POINT OF INTEREST: After reminding and rooting his audience in the truths of the gospel, Peter called them to action as obedient children in the pursuit of holiness (see 1 Pet. 1:13-15). Now that we are rooted in gospel truths, we will focus on incorporating gospel pursuits.

DAY 5

The New Life

READ EPHESIANS 4:17–5:2.

1. What does this text suggest we "put off" and "put on" (vv. 22-24)?

2. According to verse 25, what should we put away? What should we do instead?

3. Verse 31 tells us to put away all bitterness, wrath, anger, clamor, slander, and malice. Ask the Holy Spirit to reveal people toward whom you may be angry or bitter. Briefly state why.

4. How does verse 26 say we should handle anger? Why?

5. The new life in which we walk means a complete change of life. What example does verse 28 give?

6. What is God's remedy for our anger and bitterness toward others (see v. 32)?

7. How does putting away anger and bitterness allow us to live as Ephesians 5:1-2 describes?

MEDITATE ON THE FOLLOWING VERSE:

If you live according to the flesh you will die, but if by the Spirit you put to death the deeds of the body, you will live.
ROMANS 8:13

Justified by Faith!
Perfected by Law?

READ GALATIANS 2:15–3:3.

POINT OF INTEREST: Justification, according to Wayne Grudem's *Systematic Theology,* is "an instantaneous legal act of God in which he (1) thinks of our sins as forgiven and Christ's righteousness as belonging to us, and (2) declares us to be righteous in his sight."[1]

1. In verse 16 Paul assured his audience that no one will be justified "by works of the law." What does it mean to try to be justified by works of the law?

2. How can we have right standing with God (see v. 16)?

3. What was Paul dead to, according to verse 19? What was he free to do?

> My brothers, you also have died to the law through the body of
> Christ, so that you may belong to another, to him who has been
> raised from the dead, in order that we may bear fruit for God.
> **ROMANS 7:4**

4. In Galatians 2:20 Paul explained how he found that freedom. How did it affect the way he lived?

> Whoever would save his life will lose it, but whoever loses his life for my sake and the gospel's will save it.
> **MARK 8:35**

5. Can you be justified by keeping the law (see Gal. 2:21)?

> All who rely on works of the law are under a curse; for it is written, "Cursed be everyone who does not abide by all things written in the Book of the Law, and do them."
> **GALATIANS 3:10**

6. In chapter 3 why did Paul rebuke the church in Galatia?

7. Of what did he remind them?

8. Paul clearly defined how we come to faith in verse 2. How does this occur?

9. How did Paul suggest we will be "perfected" (that is, sanctified and glorified; v. 3)?

MEDITATE ON THE FOLLOWING VERSE.

It is God who works in you, both to will and to work for his good pleasure.
PHILIPPIANS 2:13

---

1. Wayne Grudem, *Systematic Theology* (Grand Rapids, MI: Zondervan, 1994), 723.

Going Deeper

1. How do you tend to view suffering? How have the precious truths of Romans 8 shaped your views?

2. Paul rebuked the church in Galatia for trying to perfect themselves through human effort alone (works). How have you tried to overcome sin by trying harder instead of trusting the Holy Spirit's work in you (grace)? Explain the difference.

3. In what ways have you made excuses or placed blame for your ungodly thoughts, behaviors, and emotions (examples: family upbringing, suffering or loss, a medical or psychological diagnosis, "the Devil made me do it," blaming others)?

Pray this prayer and spend time with the Lord.

Search me, O God, and know my heart!
Try me and know my thoughts!
And see if there be any grievous way in me,
and lead me in the way everlasting!
PSALM 139:23-24

4. What grievous ways has God revealed to you?

5. Instead of presenting yourself for unrighteousness, how can you use the same effort, enthusiasm, and creativity to present yourself to God as an instrument of righteousness (see Rom. 6:13)?

6. What evidence of the Spirit of God do you see working in you?

OVER THE NEXT THREE WEEKS YOU WILL COMPLETE YOUR ASSESSMENT.

STEP 4: We made a searching and fearless moral assessment of ourselves.

REDEEMED TRUTH FROM STEP 4: As children of God armed with the Holy Spirit and standing firm in the gospel, we engage in the spiritual battle over the reign and rule of our hearts. God set us apart for holiness, and we look to put to death the areas of our lives that keep us from reflecting Jesus Christ to a dark and dying world. We first examine the fruit in our lives (or moral symptoms). As we move through the assessment process, we will uncover the roots of any ungodly fruit (pride and idolatry) that drive our ungodly thoughts, actions, and emotions.

STEP 5: We admitted before God, ourselves, and another human being the exact nature of our wrongs.

REDEEMED TRUTH FROM STEP 5: Under the covering of God's grace, we step out in faith, leaving behind our old, self-protective ways of covering sin and hiding from God. We prayerfully come into the light, confessing our sins before God and to one another so that we may be healed.

7. What are your thoughts, concerns, and fears about completing your assessment?

8. What time will you set aside to complete your assessment? When will you meet with your mentor to share your assessment?

9. Why is it important to keep the gospel in full view as you dig into the dark places of your heart?

MEDITATE ON THE FOLLOWING VERSES AS YOU COMPLETE YOUR ASSESSMENTS.

I delivered to you as of first importance what I also received: that Christ died for our sins in accordance with the Scriptures, that he was buried, that he was raised on the third day in accordance with the Scriptures.
1 CORINTHIANS 15:3-4

ASSESSING ANGER AND ABUSE

Viewer Guide 5

COMPLETE THIS VIEWER GUIDE AS YOU WATCH THE VIDEO FOR SESSION 5.

Anger is righteous inasmuch as it captures God's _____ toward that which is producing the anger.

Unrighteous anger is when, out of pride, we react with anger to that which is interfering with our idolatrous desire and our _____.

REACTIONS TO UNRIGHTEOUS ANGER
1. We can _____ it.   2. We can _____ it.

If we are reacting unrighteously, that's a sign, a warning, an alarm that something or someone other than Jesus is _____.

We are 100 percent _____ for what comes out of us.

There is a day in the future when God, in His righteous anger, purely and perfectly will judge _____.

WHAT JESUS' VICTORY MEANS FOR THE ABUSED
1. Jesus _____ with your pain.
2. Jesus made a way not only for you to be _____ from your abuse but also where He paid the _____ for your sin that you might be made right with the Father.

HEART ISSUES OF THE ABUSED
1. A confusion of _____   2. A confusion of _____

DISTORTED DESIRES
1. We can _____ God-given desires.
2. We can _____ good desires to an unhealthy place.

LIES BEHIND A VICTIM MENTALITY
1. If this had not happened, I would be _____.
2. If God allowed this, then God is _____.
3. I'm the only one who can be _____.

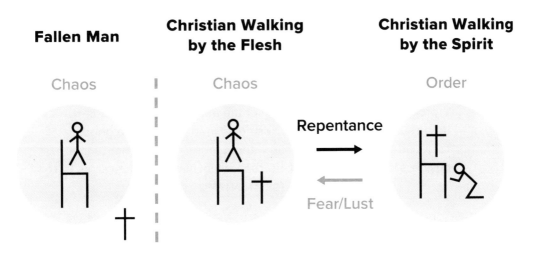

Adapted from Campus Crusade for Christ

NOTES

_____

_____

_____

_____

_____

_____

_____

_____

_____

_____

Introduction to the Assessments

A business which takes no regular inventory usually goes broke.
Taking commercial inventory is a fact-finding and a fact-facing
process. It is an effort to discover the truth about the stock-in-
trade. One objective is to disclose damaged or unsalable goods,
to get rid of them promptly and without regret. If the owner of the
business is to be successful, he cannot fool himself about values.[1]
ALCOHOLICS ANONYMOUS

Let us test and examine our ways,
and return to the Lord!
LAMENTATIONS 3:40

Over the next few weeks we will examine the current "stock-in-trade" of our hearts.
We will seek truth through the redemptive lens of the gospel as we move through
the assessment process and uncover the roots of our sin.

STEP 4: We made a searching and fearless moral assessment of ourselves.

REDEEMED TRUTH FROM STEP 4: As children of God armed with the Holy Spirit
and standing firm in the gospel, we engage in the spiritual battle over the reign and
rule of our hearts. God set us apart for holiness, and we look to put to death the
areas of our lives that keep us from reflecting Jesus Christ to a dark and dying world.
We first examine the fruit in our lives (or moral symptoms). As we move through the
assessment process, we will uncover the roots of any ungodly fruit (pride and idolatry)
that drive our ungodly thoughts, actions, and emotions.

Our hope is that through the assessment process, our hearts will come in line with
God's heart. This happens as our hearts are reconciled to His through repentance
of sin (mortification) and lives empowered by Him (vivification). God calls His children
to this heart transformation as we pursue holiness.

Preparing for Your Assessments

TIMELINE FOR COMPLETING ASSESSMENTS

We have broken the assessment down over a three-week period. The first time you work through the process, you may find it overwhelming, but focus on the major convictions that hinder your love for God and others.

Following is the suggested order for completing your assessment.[2] It is recommended that you not only set aside time to complete the assessment forms but also schedule two- to three-hour blocks each week with your mentor to share your assessments.

WEEK 5
ABUSE
ANGER & RESENTMENT

After you complete the Abuse and Anger & Resentment assessments, meet with your mentor to confess and pray through your abuse, anger, and resentment.

WEEK 6
SEXUAL IMMORALITY
GUILT & SHAME

After you complete the Sexual Immorality and Guilt & Shame assessments, meet with your mentor to confess and pray through your sexual immorality and other forms of guilt and shame.

WEEK 7
FEAR
GRIEF

After you complete the Fears & Grief assessments, meet with your mentor to confess and pray through your fears and losses.

UTILIZING YOUR MENTOR AND COMMUNITY

Your mentor is your primary support through the assessment process. Let your mentor know when you are completing your assessment so that he or she can pray for you. Call your mentor if you have any questions or difficulties.

Feel free to invite your community, group leaders, family members, and friends to pray for you during this season. It is helpful and encouraging to remember that you are not alone. Inviting others into this battle for your healing is a blessing you can extend to them.

NAMES

Record the names of people you will invite to pray for you during this assessment process.

_____

_____

_____

_____

MAKE COPIES

You may need more copies of the assessment sheets than what we provide in this book. It would be wise to go ahead and make additional copies if you think you might need them.

SET ASIDE AND GUARD THE TIME

PREPARE: Be diligent to set apart time with the Lord to pray and write. The Enemy will try to steal the time, so you must guard it.

SHARE: Schedule two or three hours each week to share your assessment with your mentor.

CREATE A FRUITFUL ENVIRONMENT

HOW YOU WORK BEST: You may prefer to write in a separate notebook, on your computer, or on the sheets provided. Later you can transfer the information to your assessment sheets or ask your mentor to help you transfer them.

WHERE YOU WORK BEST: You may prefer to do the work early in the morning or late at night. You may prefer to work in your yard, in the woods, or at your kitchen table. Create an environment conducive to meeting with the Lord.

COME TO THE LIGHT EXPECTANTLY

How free do you want to be? Honesty and thoroughness are key to assessment. You must be honest with yourself and God if you have any hope of being honest with others. This is no time to deny the truth or to superficially gloss over the issues.

> They have healed the wound of my people lightly,
>> saying, "Peace, peace,"
>> when there is no peace.
>> **JEREMIAH 6:14**

We are in a spiritual battle. Hiding in the darkness is the Enemy's domain. It is time to bring sin into the light for forgiveness and healing.

> Everyone who does wicked things hates the light and does not come to the light, lest his works should be exposed. But whoever does what is true comes to the light, so that it may be clearly seen that his works have been carried out in God.
>> **JOHN 3:20-21**

This is the message we have heard from him and proclaim to you, that God is light, and in him is no darkness at all. If we say we have fellowship with him while we walk in darkness, we lie and do not practice the truth. But if we walk in the light, as he is in the light, we have fellowship with one another, and the blood of Jesus his Son cleanses us from all sin.

1 JOHN 1:5-7

BALANCE YOUR ASSESSMENTS

We do not balance our assessments in the traditional sense of listing our good moral behavior against our bad behavior. However, we want to balance our assessments with gospel truths amid our gospel pursuits.

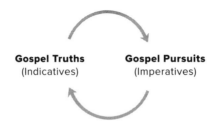

Gospel Truths
(Indicatives)

Gospel Pursuits
(Imperatives)

As we pursue holiness, we must do so from a firm foundation of who we are in Christ and all He has done and promised. We must remember what is of first importance.

I delivered to you as of first importance what I also received: that Christ died for our sins in accordance with the Scriptures, that he was buried, that he was raised on the third day in accordance with the Scriptures.

1 CORINTHIANS 15:3-4

---

1. Bob Smith and Bill Wilson, *The Big Book of Alcoholics Anonymous* (New York: Alcoholics Anonymous World Services, 2015), 64.
2. The assessment forms are modified and expanded from forms in *Joe and Charlie Big Book Study,* then viewed through a redemptive lens.

The Pattern for Completing Your Assessments

The assessment process includes both the rooting out of sin and the replanting of truth.

> The goal in assessment is not for us to identify every sin we have ever committed but to illuminate dysfunctional (sinful) patterns of relating to God and others. We want to be free of the things that rob our affections for Christ and hinder our ability to live for His kingdom purposes. Through this process we want to examine our hearts.
>
> **ASSESSMENT IS:**
> - Examining our hearts, guided by the Holy Spirit
> - Being able to identify our sins and the sinful patterns behind them
>
> **ASSESSMENT IS NOT:**
> - An attempt to document every sin
> - A one-time event

It is important to root ourselves in the gospel as we examine the darkness of our hearts. We begin by standing in the truths of the gospel—what Christ accomplished, what He is accomplishing, and what He promises to accomplish. We ask the Holy Spirit to reveal areas that hinder us from properly relating to God and others as ambassadors to a lost and dying world. We spend time writing what He reveals in our assessment. We must continually remember the gospel, believe the gospel, and stand in the gospel so that the Enemy does not cause us to stumble.

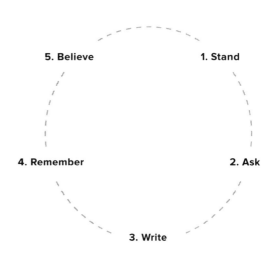

5. Believe

1. Stand

4. Remember

2. Ask

3. Write

Assessment Form Directions and Definitions

This section explains the terms found on the assessment forms so that both you and your mentor will know how to fill them out.

DIRECTIONS

1. Pray that the Holy Spirit reveals, leads, and comforts you as you fill out your assessment forms.
2. Fill out the assessment forms vertically (column by column), not horizontally (row by row). It is easier to record everything when you fill out the forms this way. Staying in the same issue too long can become overwhelming.
3. Fill out all light-blue spaces, but leave dark-blue spaces blank. You will complete the dark-blue spaces with your mentor.

DEFINITIONS

ABUSE is the misuse of anything. God created all things for His glory, and the misuse of His creation is abuse and ultimately sinful. However, there is a type of abuse that moves beyond what might be considered normative in the Christian life. This abuse is horrific, and in keeping with God's heart for the oppressed, the church must be a redemptive instrument in intervening and protecting. We cannot overcome sin independent of God. He has provided the way to overcome sin and its effects through the gospel of Jesus Christ. God does not allow abuse or any other form of suffering in the lives of His children without a redemptive purpose. In Christ, through the Holy Spirit, we can display His supremacy and victory over evil as we rise above sin, shame, and even death.

ANGER is an emotional response to a perceived wrong that demands justice. Not all anger is sinful; it can be the appropriate response to injustice. Unrighteous anger is rooted in man's attempts to meet his own idolatrous desires. Righteous anger is aligned with the Holy Spirit and flows from the heart of God in love for that which He cares about, spurring us on to gospel-centered action to eradicate evil and injustice.

GUILT can be both a state and a feeling that occurs when we have violated a law or a moral standard. We can feel guilty and not be guilty (false guilt), or we can be guilty and not feel guilty. False guilt occurs when someone besides God is the lord of our lives and their judgments matter more than His. Not feeling guilt when we are guilty is a sign of a hardened heart. Only the gospel can reconcile a heart of injustice. Life through the Holy Spirit brings conviction when we operate outside God's intended design.

SHAME is the intense feeling of being unclean, defiled, and dirty. Closely related to guilt, shame may result from the exposure of a person's own sin and depravity or from sin committed against a person's dignity. Shame is deeply rooted in identity ("I am worthless; I am dirty"). The gospel of Jesus Christ gives us a new identity and a covering for our shame. Even though we may sin or be sinned against, shame no longer rules our lives, because our identity is found in Jesus Christ.

SEX is a beautiful, sacred gift given to us by God. It is to be worshipful but not worshiped. It is to be enjoyed and celebrated within the marriage covenant as a reflection of the gospel and our union with Christ. Any sexual act that occurs outside God's intended design is sexual immorality. Beyond action alone God looks deeper to the desires and motivations of the heart. Only through the gospel will God align our hearts with His purposes for this beautiful, sacred gift.

FEAR is an emotional response to a perceived threat or danger. Spiritually, healthy fear is the fear of the Lord. To fear the Lord is to worship Him alone and is the source of all wisdom and understanding. The absence of the fear of the Lord is the height of foolishness and leads to destruction. Outside the gospel we live our lives from a self-centered fear that seeks to meet our own perceived needs. As the Holy Spirit reveals this foolishness, we come under the compassion and care of our loving Father. He knows best in providing, protecting, and directing our lives according to His plan and purpose for His glory and our good.

GRIEF is a natural response to loss and is not sinful. When we grieve, we can do so knowing that we stand in the loving arms of God the Father. Grief in this context is always hopeful because we know that God is making all things new. Grief outside the gospel leaves us to cope through self-generated means and with false hope or no hope at all. Grief can become complicated when we idolize what we lost.

What Part of Self Was Threatened?

The following definitions will be useful to you and your mentor in determining which part of self was hurt or threatened in the Resentment, Sexual Immorality, and Guilt & Shame assessments. For each person or circumstance you identify on these assessments, place a check mark in any boxes that apply. In almost every instance several boxes will be checked for the same person or circumstance.

DEFINITIONS

SELF-ESTEEM: The desire for love, worth, and value

PERSONAL RELATIONSHIPS: The desire to belong and have meaningful relationships

MATERIAL SECURITY: The desire to feel materially secure or gain material wealth

EMOTIONAL SECURITY: The desire or drive for peace of mind and emotional security

SEXUAL RELATIONS/SEXUALITY: Sexual desires

AMBITIONS: Future plans and hopes in any of the previous areas

EXAMPLES

The following examples illustrate how to identify which part of self is being hurt or threatened.

GUILT AND SHAME: "I feel shame over being raped. I feel worthless now, as if no one will ever love me [self-esteem]. Being raped has made it difficult to date [sexual relations/sexuality] because all I think about is how dirty I feel. I fear that I will never be able to have sex [sexual ambitions] in a healthy way."

RESENTMENT: "I am angry at my mother for taking me out of her will. I feel that she doesn't care about me [self-esteem] at all, and I was counting on that money to pay my debt [material security]. I am convinced that she loves my sister more than me [emotional security], and her favoritism has always caused my sister and me to be estranged [personal relationships]."

SEXUAL IMMORALITY: "When I watched pornography, it made me feel powerful [self-esteem] and met my sexual needs [sexual relations/sexuality]. It also allowed me intimacy without having to be vulnerable [emotional security]."

ABUSE ASSESSMENT

ABUSE Abuse is the misuse of anything. It is horrific. God created all things for His glory, and misuse of His creation is abuse and ultimately sinful. All sin is abusive, and sin against others is undeserved for those whom it affects. For our purposes we want to limit our assessments to those things that are overtly abusive or have wounded us in a way that impairs how we relate to God and others.

GOSPEL TRUTH: Before starting the assessment, take time to read the following verses and to summarize the character and promises of God.

MATTHEW 15:1-14

ROMANS 6

ROMANS 8

GALATIANS 2:15–3:3

EPHESIANS 4:17–5:2

REVELATION 21–22

INSTRUCTIONS

GOSPEL PURSUIT

Prayerfully consider whether the following areas may have been abuse in your life.

Physical abuse—assault, neglect
Sexual abuse—date rape, rape, molestation, incest
Emotional abuse—shaming, emotional blackmail, guilt trips, emotional incest, neglect
Power/authority abuse—coercion, intimidation, church, workplace, military
Verbal abuse—threatening, belittling, ridiculing, demeaning, name-calling
Ritual abuse—satanic-ritual abuse, occult ritual abuse

THE ASSESSMENT FORM

SOURCE: List the people, institutions, or principles that may have been abusive toward you.

THE CAUSE: Specifically explain what happened to you. Some people may prefer writing a narrative, while others may prefer bullet points.

TYPE OF ABUSE: Check the type of abuse.

RESIDUAL EFFECTS: Check whether the fruit of shame, resentment, fear/anxiety, guilt, or grief is currently present in your life. Transfer the situation to the corresponding assessment sheets. For example, if you listed an uncle for physical abuse that has resulted in shame, add his name to your Guilt and Shame assessments. You will deal with that situation on both assessments.

REMEMBER: If you have been in an abusive relationship, renounce the lie that you are responsible for the abuse itself. You cannot cause another person to sin.

MY RESPONSE

Think about the following questions and indicate your response to the abuse.

- How have I responded to the abuse?
- In what ways have I attempted to deal with these wounds?
- Have I suppressed the abuse?
- To whom or what have I turned other than God in order to cope?

STOP: You will complete the "Exact nature of my wrongs" section with your mentor.

ABUSE ASSESSMENT FORM

Rejoice not over me, O my enemy; when I fall, I shall rise; when I sit in darkness, the LORD will be a light to me. **MICAH 7:8**

Source	Cause	Type of Abuse					
		Sexual	Emotional	Power/authority	Ritualistic	Verbal	Physical

Shame	Resentment	Fear/anxiety	Grief/loss	Guilt	Regarding guilt: renounce the lie that I am responsible for the abuse.	My Response	Self-centered	Self-seeking	Frightened	Dishonest	Inconsiderate	Other

If any of these are currently present in my life regarding this situation, add to other assessments.

Exact nature of my wrongs, faults, and mistakes (to complete with mentor)

PRAYER PROMPTS

Abuse

After you complete your assessment, confessing to God and to your mentor, walk through the prayer below. You may pray the prayer as written or use the elements of the prayer in your own words.

NOTE: Pray through each item, person, or circumstance in the assessment.

PRAYER FOR ABUSE

Heavenly Father, I thank You that You are the God who sees. I thank You that in my darkest moments You were there. I thank You that when no one else heard my cries, You did. You sent Your Son to this world to rescue me and give me life. Jesus, You know well my pain, because You Yourself suffered much at the hands of sinners. I pray that You will teach me through your Spirit to love as You love. Thank You for rescuing me from the dominion of darkness and bringing me with You into eternity. I thank You that I am no longer a victim but more than a conqueror through the cross. In Christ I am cleansed. I pray, in the name of Jesus Christ, that You will begin to heal any emotional, spiritual, mental, relational, or physical damage done as a result of this abuse in my life, as well as any other people affected, for Your glory and Your namesake. Help me not to focus on the way people have treated me but instead on what You have given me. Show me how to be an instrument of Your redeeming love in this situation. [Take a moment to pray for the abuser.] In Jesus' name, amen.

ELEMENTS OF THIS PRAYER

- Acknowledge that God sees, knows, and cares about our darkest moments.
- Thank Him that He sent Christ to rescue us.
- Acknowledge that Christ understands, because He Himself suffered, and that the Holy Spirit will teach you to love as He loves.
- Thank God that we are no longer enslaved to darkness and that we will spend eternity with Him.
- Acknowledge that we are more than conquerors in Christ (see Rom. 8:37) and are no longer victims.
- Pray for healing.
- Ask God to help you focus on what you have been given eternally rather than on what has been taken from you in this life.
- Pray for wisdom in being an instrument of His redeeming love in this situation.
- Pray for the abuser.

ANGER AND RESENTMENT ASSESSMENT

To understand resentment, we must first understand anger.

ANGER is an emotional response to a perceived wrong that demands justice. Not all anger is sinful; it can be the appropriate response to injustice. Unrighteous anger is rooted in man's attempts to meet his own idolatrous desires. Righteous anger is aligned with the Holy Spirit and flows from the heart of God in love for that which He cares about, spurring us on to gospel-centered action to eradicate evil and injustice.

Unresolved anger may lead to resentment.

GOSPEL TRUTH: Before starting the assessment, take time to read the following verses and to summarize the character and promises of God.

LUKE 6:35-36

JOHN 5:30

ROMANS 12:19

HEBREWS 12:15

INSTRUCTIONS

GOSPEL PURSUIT

Begin the Anger & Resentment assessment by prayerfully considering areas of unresolved resentment toward yourself, God, or others. The goal is not to record every resentment you have ever had but the resentments that currently hinder your love of God and others. Do not give the Enemy a foothold by intentionally leaving sin in darkness.

It may be helpful to get a piece of paper and brainstorm, asking God to help you call to mind any people you might have resentment toward if they walked into the room. The cause may be something someone did or failed to do. You may also resent a situation, an institution, or even an idea.

PEOPLE

- God/Jesus
- Clergy/pastors
- Parents/grandparents (step)
- Siblings (step)
- Extended family
- In-laws
- Adopted/foster family
- Husbands/wives
- Boyfriends/girlfriends
- Babysitters
- Playmates
- Childhood friends
- Family friends
- Middle-school/high-school friends
- College classmates (fraternity/sorority)
- Current friends
- Teachers/counselors/principals/coaches
- Employers
- Coworkers
- Creditors
- Police/probation/parole officers
- Judges/lawyers
- Church members
- Cult members
- Gang members
- Sports-team members
- Acquaintances/neighbors
- Politicians/civic leaders
- Counselors/therapists/psychiatrists
- Doctors/nurses/aides

INSTITUTIONS

- Religion/church
- Marriage/family
- Recovery programs
- Treatment centers
- Judicial/correctional
- Government
- Education
- Hospitals
- Mental health
- Corporations

SPIRITUAL PRINCIPLES
- Authority
- Confession
- Repentance
- Heaven/hell
- Election
- Predestination

- Law
- Sin
- Sickness/death
- Restitution
- Divorce/separation
- Reconciliation

THE ASSESSMENT FORM

SOURCE: List those toward whom you are resentful or those who have hurt you.

THE CAUSE: Explain why you are resentful and list the specific action done to you. Some people may prefer writing a narrative, while others may prefer bullet points.

THE EFFECT: Describe the effect of this resentment on your life and your relationships.

WHAT PART OF SELF WAS HURT OR THREATENED?

There are four major categories in which you may identify hurt or threat:

- Social
- Security

- Sexual
- Ambitions

You may view these four major categories as a current threat at the time the incident occurred or as a threat to a future hope (ambitions). In other words, you could be resentful toward someone who intruded in a current, personal relationship or threatened a future hope or ambition.

KEY QUESTIONS

SOCIAL

Indicate whether this offense hurt or threatened my relationships, specifically in these two areas:

Self-esteem: Did this offense hurt or threaten my sense of worth, value, confidence, identity, etc.?

Personal relationships: Did this offense hurt or threaten my sense of belonging or the relationships I value? Did it affect the way I relate to others?

SECURITY

Indicate whether this offense hurt or threatened my sense of security in one of two areas:

Materially: Did this offense hurt or threaten me financially or materially?

Emotionally: Did this offense hurt or threaten me emotionally?

SEXUAL

Did this offense hurt or threaten my sexual relations or sexuality?

AMBITIONS

Did this a offense hurt or threaten my future hopes and plans?

Again, rather than a current threat, the Ambitions assessment recognizes that we often become resentful because our plans for the future (hopes) have been interrupted (social, material, emotional, or sexual ideals). Examples: "I never thought I would be divorced." "I was hoping to marry her."

STOP: You will complete the "Exact nature of my wrongs" section with your mentor.

ANGER AND RESENTMENT ASSESSMENT FORM

See to it that no one fails to obtain the grace of God; that no "root of bitterness" springs up and causes trouble, and by it many become defiled. **HEBREWS 12:15**

Source	Cause	Effect

What part of self was hurt or threatened?

Social		Security				Exact nature of my wrongs, faults, and mistakes (to complete with mentor)					
Self-esteem	Personal Relationships	Material	Emotional	Sexual	Ambitions	Self-centered	Self-seeking	Frightened	Dishonest	Inconsiderate	Other

Anger and Resentment

After you complete your assessment, confessing to God and to your mentor, walk through the prayer below. You may pray the prayer as written or use the elements of the prayer in your own words.

NOTE: Pray through each item, person, or circumstance in the assessment.

PRAYER FOR RESENTMENT TOWARD OTHERS

Heavenly Father, I acknowledge that [person's name] is not exempt from the fall and the effects of sin. Though I do not like the symptoms of this spiritual disease or the ways it has affected me, he [or she], like me, is a sinner. I confess that I have stood in judgment of _____ for _____. Forgive me, Father, for allowing bitterness and resentment to reside in my heart, preventing my ability to be an instrument of Your redeeming love. As You, Father, have extended your grace to me through Jesus Christ, I ask the Holy Spirit to enable me to reflect Christ in this situation. Today I, as an unrighteous judge, turn this offense over to you, my righteous Judge and King. I trust in Your will and Your plan and choose to live in the freedom You have promised. How may I be an ambassador of your love, peace, and truth in this situation? I pray in the name of Jesus Christ that You will, for Your namesake and glory, heal any damage done as a result of this offense in my life, as well as any others who may have been affected. [Finish your prayer by praying for this person according to his or her needs.] In Jesus' name, amen.

ELEMENTS OF THIS PRAYER
- Humble yourself as a fellow sinner.
- Confess specific resentment.
- Ask for forgiveness for harboring bitterness .
- Ask for the Holy Spirit's help in being Christlike.
- Turn the offense over to God.
- Ask for wisdom on how to best steward this relationship for God's kingdom purposes.
- Pray for healing.
- Pray for the other person.

PRAYER FOR RESENTMENT TOWARD SELF

Heavenly Father, forgive me for the ways I have attempted to find righteousness apart from the work of Your Son. By standing outside myself, elevating myself and judging myself for my actions, emotions, and behavior and therefore hating myself, I have attempted to deal with my shortcomings according to the law rather than Your grace. I tend to punish myself when I break my standards, seeking some sense of justification. In doing so, I try to deal with my sin independent of You and remain in self-imposed bondage. I have placed myself above You as judge. Today I come humbly before You so that I can come under the waterfall of Your grace. Thank You for Your Son, Jesus, and the freedom that grace brings. In Jesus' name, amen.

ELEMENTS OF THIS PRAYER
- Ask for forgiveness for attempting to find righteousness apart from Christ.
- Confess attempts to deal with shortcomings according to the law rather than grace.
- Repent of punishment and judgment of yourself in an attempt to seek justification.
- Acknowledge the self-imposed bondage you have created in attempting to deal with your sin apart from Christ.
- Ask to stand under His grace and the freedom He brings.
- Offer thanksgiving for Jesus.

PRAYER FOR RESENTMENT TOWARD GOD

Heavenly Father, I confess my resentment toward You for _____. I ask Your forgiveness for my pride, standing in judgment of a good, perfect, just, and holy God who can see the eternal perspective, while I can see only what is right before me. Help me, by the power of Your Holy Spirit, to trust You and remember that Your plans are to bless me and not to harm me, to give me hope and a future. In Jesus' name, amen.

ELEMENTS OF THIS PRAYER
- Confess specific resentment.
- Ask for forgiveness for standing in judgment.
- Humbly acknowledge that you do not knows what God knows.
- Repent of not trusting God and His eternal perspective.
- Give thanks for the assurance God provides His children.

Going Deeper

> Be angry, and do not sin;
> ponder in your own hearts on your beds, and be silent.
> **PSALM 4:4**

1. When someone wrongs you, how do you typically respond? Give examples.

READ MATTHEW 5:21-22.

2. What is the point of Jesus' interpretation of the command not to murder?

READ ROMANS 12:9-21.

3. Most of us respond to evil by taking revenge. Such a response can take on many forms. Some people withhold love by withdrawing (becoming passive or suppressing our hurt). Others respond aggressively by yelling, throwing tantrums, or doing something worse. How are we commanded to respond to evil?

READ MATTHEW 5:38-41.

4. What examples did Jesus give for responding to personal offenses?

POINT OF INTEREST: The response Jesus taught is not passive or aggressive but an act of generosity that allows the offender the opportunity to see his or her wrong.

READ MATTHEW 5:23-24.

5. What should we do if we remember that our brother has something against us?

READ JAMES 1:19-20.

6. What is man's anger unable to produce? Give examples of this truth in your life.

READ MATTHEW 18:15-17.

7. What are we to do if our brother sins against us?

READ EPHESIANS 4:26-27.

8. What wisdom should we take away from these verses?

9. Based on today's discussion, what might the Lord be trying to tell you through His Word?

NOTES

ASSESSING SEX, GUILT, AND SHAME

Viewer Guide 6

COMPLETE THIS VIEWER GUIDE AS YOU WATCH THE VIDEO FOR SESSION 6.

When God created sex, He created it to be _____.

If the goal for sex is to have our own satisfactions met, then ultimately, it will become _____.

Pornea: any form of _____ _____ that does not reflect God's intended desire

God does not offer intimacy to those He's not in _____ with.

The two should become one and never be _____ again.

Real guilt: I have done something _____.

False guilt: I didn't do anything wrong, but I _____ like I did something wrong.

Hard-heartedness: I did something wrong, and I should feel the weight of that, but I completely _____ it.

Shame: I'm defiled. I'm dirty. It's not that I did something wrong; it's that I _____ wrong.

Justification: I am guilty, but the Lord has declared me _____.

Adoption: Your identity has been conferred from being a simple and depraved man or woman to being a _____ of God.

When the Lord adopts us, we're no longer carrying the shame of that old identity. We've been made _____.

Sex is a beautiful and sacred gift given to us by God. It is to be worshipful but not _____.

Two Heart Issues

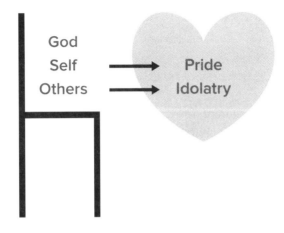

God
Self
Others

Pride
Idolatry

NOTES

_____

_____

_____

_____

_____

_____

_____

_____

_____

_____

_____

SEXUAL-IMMORALITY ASSESSMENT

SEX is a beautiful, sacred gift given to us by God. It is to be worshipful but not worshiped. It is to be enjoyed and celebrated within the marriage covenant as a reflection of the gospel and our union with Christ. Any sexual act that occurs outside God's intended design is sexual immorality. Beyond action alone God looks deeper to the desires and motivations of the heart. Only through the gospel will God align our hearts with His purposes for this beautiful, sacred gift.

GOSPEL TRUTH: Before starting the assessment, take time to read the following verses and to summarize the character and promises of God.

JOEL 2:25

MICAH 7:18-20

1 CORINTHIANS 10:13

1 JOHN 3:2-3

INSTRUCTIONS

Flee from sexual immorality. Every other sin a person commits is
outside the body, but the sexually immoral person sins against his
own body. Or do you not know that your body is a temple of the Holy
Spirit within you, whom you have from God? You are not your own,
for you were bought with a price. So glorify God in your body.
1 CORINTHIANS 6:18-20

I will restore to you the years
that the swarming locust has eaten.
JOEL 2:25

GOSPEL PURSUIT

Being the Sexual-Immorality assessment by prayerfully considering areas of sexual
immorality as a subset of guilt and shame. Identify activities that grieve God's heart
and currently burden you. How have you participated in sex outside God's intended
design? Feel free to add to the list.

- Premarital sex
- Adultery
- Homosexuality
- Promiscuity
- Lust
- Fantasizing
- Pornography

- Prostitution
- Sexual abuse
- Self-sex/masturbation
- Phone/cybersex
- Bestiality
- Sexual enticement

THE ASSESSMENT FORM

WHO/WHAT

Whom or what have I engaged sexually outside God's intended design?

THE CAUSE

List the specific actions.

THE EFFECT

Describe the effects on your life and the lives of others.

WHAT PART OF SELF WAS THREATENED OR SEEKING SATISFACTION?

Remember, a good desire becomes a lust when we are willing to sin to get it.

There are four major categories in which you may identify sexual immorality:

• Social
• Security
• Sexual
• Ambitions

KEY QUESTIONS

Prayerfully consider which of these desires you were attempting to satisfy when you engaged in this activity. Examples: "I wanted him to like me" (emotional security) or "If I could be with that girl, then I must be important" (self-esteem, treating women like trophies).

SOCIAL

Identify whether I was seeking social satisfaction, specifically in these two areas:

Self-esteem: Was I driven by a desire to build my self-esteem, self-confidence, value, or self-worth?
Personal relationships: Was I seeking acceptance, status, or belonging? Or was I responding to rejection?

SECURITY

Identify whether I was seeking security in one of these two areas:

Material: Was I driven by my desire for material security (money, a place to stay, a nice dinner)?
Emotional: Was I driven by my desire for emotional security (love, peace)?

SEXUAL

Was I seeking to satisfy my God-given desire for sex or pleasure outside His design?

AMBITIONS

Was there a perceived threat to my future plans for what I was seeking in any one of these areas?

STOP: You will complete the "Exact nature of my wrongs" section with your mentor.

SEXUAL-IMMORALITY ASSESSMENT FORM

Flee from sexual immorality. ... Your body is a temple of the Holy Spirit. ... You are not your own, for you were bought with a price. So glorify God in your body. **1 CORINTHIANS 6:18-20**

Who/What	Cause	Effect

What part of self was threatened or seeking satisfaction?						Exact nature of my wrongs, faults, and mistakes (to complete with mentor)					
Social		Security									
Self-esteem	Personal relationships	Material	Emotional	Sexual	Ambitions	Self-centered	Self-seeking	Frightened	Dishonest	Inconsiderate	Other

Sexual Immorality

After you complete your assessment, confessing to God and to your mentor, walk through the prayer below. You may pray the prayer as written or use the elements of the prayer in your own words.

NOTE: Pray through each item, person, or circumstance in the assessment.

PRAYER FOR SEXUAL IMMORALITY

Heavenly Father, I realize that sex is sacred. It is a beautiful picture of oneness reserved exclusively for one man and one woman within the context of the marriage covenant. Sex is a gift from You that is intended to glorify You. It is the mingling of souls. Lord, I confess today that I have sinned and operated outside Your intended design for this holy endeavor by _____. Father, forgive me. I have given intimate parts of myself to another. Lord, I long to glorify You. I ask that You will restore to me a right view of sex. I pray, in the name of Jesus Christ, that for Your namesake and by Your power, You will heal the damage done as a result of this situation in my life, as well as any damage in other lives that have been affected. I pray You will break any soul ties related to this sin. I trust in the redemptive work of Christ and His covering for my shame. I pray that You will remove or help me take captive the images and emotions tied to these events and prevent me from fantasizing or taking pride in things that grieve Your heart. Through the cross of Christ I am made clean. In Jesus name', amen.

GUILT AND SHAME ASSESSMENT

GUILT can be both a state and a feeling that occurs when we have violated a law or a moral standard. We can feel guilty and not be guilty (false guilt), or we can be guilty and not feel guilty. False guilt occurs when someone besides God is the lord of our lives and their judgments matter more than His. Not feeling guilt when we are guilty is a sign of a hardened heart. Only the gospel can reconcile a heart of injustice. Life through the Holy Spirit brings conviction when we operate outside God's intended design.

SHAME is the intense feeling of being unclean, defiled, and dirty. Closely related to guilt, shame may result from the exposure of a person's own sin and depravity or from sin committed against a person's dignity. Shame is deeply rooted in identity ("I am worthless; I am dirty"). The gospel of Jesus Christ gives us a new identity and a covering for our shame. Even though we may sin or be sinned against, shame no longer rules our lives, because our identity is found in Jesus Christ.

GOSPEL TRUTH: Before starting the assessment, take time to read the following verses and to summarize the character and promises of God.

PSALM 34:15-18

PSALM 34:22

PSALM 71:1-3

HEBREWS 4:15-16

1 JOHN 1:7

1 JOHN 1:9

INSTRUCTIONS

GOSPEL PURSUIT

Begin the Guilt & Shame assessments by prayerfully considering areas of unresolved guilt and shame. Guilt can be a feeling or a state. You may feel guilty and not be guilty or vice versa. The goal is not to record every sin you committed or every sin committed against you but the sins that currently burden you or need to be reconciled with God. Do not give the Enemy a foothold by intentionally leaving sin in darkness.

GUILT

- Abortion (or the approval of one)
- Abuse (verbal, sexual, physical, spiritual, authority, emotional)
- Addictions (gambling, shopping, sexual, drug, alcohol, food, etc.)
- Adultery
- Anger (violence, fighting, murder)
- Anything or anyone you put first over God (idolatry)
- Cheating
- Complaining
- Controlling
- Coveting (railing against God's provision in your life)
- Critical
- Dishonesty, lying, inauthenticity
- Divorce (biblical or otherwise)
- Fear/anxiety
- Gossiping
- Lust (can be for things other than sex)
- Jealousy
- Misleading others
- Neglect
- Promiscuity
- Rebelliousness
- Self-righteousness
- Selfishness
- Sexual sin (broken out separately on the sexual assessment)
- Slandering
- Slothful (not just sitting on the couch but neglecting the important areas of life)
- Stealing (from family, stores, the government, companies, church, friends)
- Quarrelsome
- Vandalism
- Violence
- Voyeurism

SHAME

- Dirty feeling
- Unclean
- Defiled
- Deep desire to hide
- Inability to connect
- Unworthy
- Alienated
- Damaged
- Unlovable
- Infected

THE ASSESSMENT FORM

THE CAUSE: Specifically, what caused the shame or guilt? List the action that you did or that was done to you. Some people may prefer writing a narrative, while others may prefer bullet points.

WHO WAS HURT? List those affected.

THE EFFECT: Describe the effects of this guilt and shame on your life.

WHAT PART OF SELF WAS THREATENED OR SEEKING SATISFACTION?
Remember, a good desire becomes a lust when we are willing to sin to get it.

There are four major categories in which you may identify guilt or shame:

• Social
• Security
• Sexual
• Ambitions

Each of these areas of self may have been threatened or seeking satisfaction at the time of the incident. We say "may" because we can experience shame when we are not guilty of sin but instead are sinned against and defiled, marring our God-given dignity.

KEY QUESTIONS

SOCIAL

Identify whether there was a perceived threat to my social identity (fear) or whether I was seeking to satisfy my perceived social "needs" in one of these specific areas:

Self-esteem: Was I seeking love, value, worth, or identity from others (lust), or was my sense of identity, worth, value, or esteem threatened by others (fear)?

Personal relationships: Was I seeking to belong (lust), or was there a perceived threat to my personal relationships (fear)?

SECURITY

Identify whether there was a perceived threat to my security (fear) or whether I was seeking to satisfy my perceived "need" for security (lust) in one of these areas:

Materially: Was I seeking material security (lust), or was there a perceived threat to my material security (fear)?

Emotionally: Was I seeking emotional security (lust), or was there a perceived threat to my sense of emotional security or peace (fear)?

SEXUAL

Was there a perceived threat to my sexuality (fear), or was I seeking sexual satisfaction (lust)?

AMBITIONS

Was there a perceived threat to my future plans for what I was seeking in any one of these areas?

STOP: You will complete the "Exact nature of my wrongs" section with your mentor.

GUILT AND SHAME ASSESSMENT FORM

I do not nullify the grace of God, for if righteousness were through the law, then Christ died for no purpose. **GALATIANS 2:21**

Cause	Who Was Hurt?	Effect

What part of self was threatened or seeking satisfaction?						Exact nature of my wrongs, faults, and mistakes (to complete with mentor)					
Social		Security									
Self-esteem	Personal relationships	Material	Emotional	Sexual	Ambitions	Self-centered	Self-seeking	Frightened	Dishonest	Inconsiderate	Other

NOTES

137

PRAYER PROMPTS

Guilt and Shame

After you complete your assessment, confessing to God and to your mentor, walk through the prayer below. You may pray the prayer as written or use the elements of the prayer in your own words.

NOTE: Pray through each item, person, or circumstance in the assessment.

PRAYER FOR GUILT AND SHAME (AS A RESULT OF MY SIN)

Heavenly Father, today I confess that my attempts to deal with my guilt and shame by covering them with the works of my hands and hiding in darkness have failed. I come before Your throne and ask for Your forgiveness for [name the sin]. I thank You that when I come before You, hiding nothing, and trust solely in the sufficiency of Christ, I receive the covering of Your grace. I pray in the name of Jesus Christ that, by Your power, You will heal the damage done in my life as a result of this situation, as well as any damage in other lives that have been affected, and lead me to faithful reconciliation in this situation. In Jesus' name, amen.

ELEMENTS OF THIS PRAYER
- Confess the attempt to deal with guilt and shame apart from the cross of Christ.
- Confess sin and ask for forgiveness.
- Acknowledge receiving God's grace and express gratitude for the sufficiency of Christ's payment.
- Pray for the healing and restoration of the other people affected.
- Ask what needs to be done to rectify the situation.

When you receive God's forgiveness but fail to forgive yourself, you kick God off the throne and set yourself up as the higher authority. In essence you count the cross of Jesus as nothing. Repent and accept Christ's forgiveness. Walk in the freedom of knowing that Jesus' blood is sufficient. Thank Him.

PRAYER FOR SHAME (AS A RESULT OF ANOTHER'S SIN)

Heavenly Father, today I confess that my attempts to deal with my shame by covering it with the works of my hands and hiding in darkness have failed. Because I now trust in the cleansing work of the cross of our Lord Jesus Christ, I now step out of the darkness and into the light. Though _____ may have _____, there is nothing that the resurrecting power of Jesus cannot overcome. Through the cross of Christ I am made clean. I pray in the name of Jesus Christ that, by Your power, You will heal the damage done in my life as a result of this situation, as well as any damage in other lives that have been affected. In Jesus' name, amen.

ELEMENTS OF THIS PRAYER
- Acknowledge insufficiency in attempting to deal with shame apart from the cross of Christ.
- Bring to light the specific sin by naming the person and what he or she did.
- Acknowledge that there is no sin that the resurrection power of Christ cannot overcome.
- Acknowledge having been made clean through the cross of Christ.
- Pray for the healing of those affected.

ELEMENTS OF THIS PRAYER
- Acknowledge the sacred beauty and gift that sex is within its intended design.
- Acknowledge the spiritual reality that takes place when two people join together.
- Confess sin specifically.
- Ask for forgiveness.
- Express your desire to bring glory to God.
- Pray for a restored view of sex.
- Pray for healing.
- Pray for the breaking of soul ties.
- Express trust in God's work in you.
- Ask for help in taking your thoughts captive, making them obedient to the will of Christ, and ask for the removal of images and emotions related to the event.
- Acknowledge having been cleansed through the blood of Jesus.

Going Deeper

1. How do you tend to view sex? Do you view it as dirty, delightful, gross, or a gift? Why?

2. According to Genesis 2 (life before the fall), who gives the gift of sex? What do you think the Giver intends for the gift?

3. Who owns and holds authority over sex? What context has God given for enjoying the gift?

4. Would past evidence support that you tend to despise the gift, worship the gift, or worship the Giver?

READ 1 CORINTHIANS 6:12-20.

5. What arguments about sexual immorality did the Corinthian church make, and how did Paul respond?

This is the will of God, your sanctification:
that you abstain from sexual immorality.
1 THESSALONIANS 4:3

6. According to 1 Corinthians 6:12-20, to whom are we to give ultimate glory with our bodies?

7. What gospel imperative (command) did Paul use in dealing with sexual immorality (see v. 18)?

8. In what gospel indicative (truth) did Paul root his command (see v. 19)?

9. What words describe the action of using a body for your own sexual pleasure against the owner's will?

You have heard that it was said, "You shall not commit adultery."
But I say to you that everyone who looks at a woman with lustful
intent has already committed adultery with her in his heart.
MATTHEW 5:27-28

10. Many people ask, "How far is too far?" in terms of sexual behavior. How did Jesus redirect the conversation away from outward appropriateness? In light of His teaching, how far is too far?

11. In Matthew 5:20 Jesus said unless we have a righteousness that exceeds the outward righteousness of the Pharisees, we will not enter the kingdom of God. How is the gospel the only hope for a superior righteousness?

12. How can the sexual union of a man and a woman in marriage reflect the gospel or the relationship between Christ and His bride?

13. How can we apply gospel hope to those who have been defiled, either willingly or unwillingly, through sexual immorality?

ASSESSING FEAR, ANXIETY, AND GRIEF

Viewer Guide 7

COMPLETE THIS VIEWER GUIDE AS YOU WATCH THE VIDEO FOR SESSION 7.

Comfort: to come to someone's aid, to encourage, to come _____ someone

Some suffering is as a result of our own _____. Some comes from being sinned against. And other suffering is just the tragic result of a _____ world.

THREE TRUTHS ABOUT GOD
1. God _____ you.
2. God is _____.
3. God is _____ and purposeful.

If you're under the covering of God's grace, there is literally nothing to _____.

Part of God's call on all of our lives is that we may be called at times to go places where we will experience suffering for His _____.

You can't lose anything that's _____, and you can't keep anything from here.

The two most primitive expressions of a prideful heart are _____ and _____.

Lusts seek to control and _____. Fears seek to control and _____.

We have our dependence not on us and our abilities to provide for ourselves but rather on the God who tells us He _____ us and who is _____.

If I am trusting in the Lord, nothing else can _____ me; nothing else can raise _____ in me.

STAGES OF GRIEF
1. _____
2. _____ and resentment
3. _____
4. _____ and alienation
5. _____

A BIBLICAL UNDERSTANDING OF GRIEF

1. We move from denial to candor.
2. We move from anger to lament—getting honest with God.
3. We move from bargaining to crying out to God—asking God for help.
4. We move from depression and alienation to comfort—receiving God's help.
5. We move from regrouping and pushing forward in our own strength to waiting and trusting with faith when God says, "Not yet."
6. We move from deadening to wailing—groaning with hope.
7. We move from despairing and doubting to weaving—perceiving with grace.
8. We move from digging cisterns to worshiping God, the Redeemer.[1]

---

1. Adapted from Robert Kellemen, *God's Healing for Life's Losses* (Winona Lake, IN: BMH, 2010).

NOTES

_____

_____

_____

_____

_____

_____

_____

_____

_____

_____

_____

FEAR ASSESSMENT

FEAR is an emotional response to a perceived threat or danger. Spiritually, healthy fear is the fear of the Lord. To fear the Lord is to worship Him alone and is the source of all wisdom and understanding. The absence of the fear of the Lord is the height of foolishness and leads to destruction. Outside the gospel we live our lives from a self-centered fear that seeks to meet our own perceived needs. As the Holy Spirit reveals this foolishness, we come under the compassion and care of our loving Father. He knows best in providing, protecting, and directing our lives according to His plan and purpose for His glory and our good.

GOSPEL TRUTH: Before starting the assessment, take time to read the following verses and to summarize the character and promises of God.

PSALM 73:24-26

PSALM 91:9-16

PSALM 118:6

PHILIPPIANS 4:5-6

INSTRUCTIONS

GOSPEL PURSUIT

Begin the Fear assessment by prayerfully considering whether the following fears are part of your life. Feel free to add to the list.

- Fear of God/Jesus
- Fear of man
- Fear of losing a loved one
- Fear of abandonment
- Fear of intimacy/relationships
- Fear of rejection/loneliness
- Fear of authority (parents, teachers, police, boss, etc.)
- Fear of unemployment, creditors, financial ruin
- Fear of sobriety/relapse

- Fear of being found out
- Fear of people different from me
- Fear of conflict/confrontation
- Fear of success/failure
- Fear of getting old/body image
- Fear of losing control
- Fear of illness/germs
- Fear of pain/death
- Fear of change
- Fear of the unknown/the future

THE ASSESSMENT FORM

FEAR
List your fear or anxiety.

THE EFFECT
Describe the effect of this fear on your life. How do you respond to fear?

THE CIRCUMSTANCES
Describe any circumstances that have contributed to these fears.

STOP: You will complete the final sections with your mentor.

FEAR ASSESSMENT FORM

I, the LORD your God, hold your right hand; it is I who say to you, "Fear not, I am the one who helps you." **ISAIAH 41:13**

Fear	Effect

Circumstance

What influences or circumstances contributed to this fear?

Where is my treasure?
(Complete with mentor.)

Review Matthew 6:19-34.

GRIEF ASSESSMENT

GRIEF is a natural response to loss and is not sinful. When we grieve, we can do so knowing that we stand in the loving arms of God the Father. Grief in this context is always hopeful because we know that God is making all things new. Grief outside the gospel leaves us to cope through self-generated means and with false hope or no hope at all. Grief can become complicated when we idolize what we lost.

GOSPEL TRUTH: Before starting the assessment, take time to read the following verses and to summarize the character and promises of God.

PSALM 100

ISAIAH 40:28-31

EZEKIEL 37:1-6

JOHN 6:49-51

JOHN 10:9-10

COLOSSIANS 3:1-2

INSTRUCTIONS

Grief can be very traumatic and often comes with painful emotions and difficult decisions. Everyone reacts and handles suffering in different ways. There are no hard and fast rules for how to handle loss; however, there are truths to remember, as well as tools and expectations to help navigate you through this season.

- You are not alone. God is near. Walk closely with your community and family.
- Do not avoid the painful reality of your loss by turning to quick fixes instead of entrusting yourself to God.
- Do not use biblical truths to avoid heartfelt cries to the Lord (for example, "God uses all things for our good").
- Do not neglect being a good steward of your body, mind, and spirit.
- Milestones can be difficult (anniversaries, birthdays, weddings, vacations).

> The LORD is near to the brokenhearted
> and saves the crushed in spirit.
> **PSALM 34:18**

GOSPEL PURSUIT

Begin the Grief assessment by prayerfully considering areas of unresolved grief. Feel free to add to the list.

- Death of a loved one
- Divorce
- Infertility
- Illness/injury
- Loss of relationship
- Loss of job
- Extended singleness
- Loss of possession(s)
- Loss of identity (homosexuality, cults, etc.)
- Loss of community
- Wayward child
- Difficulties in marriage
- Grief over own sin or consequences

THE ASSESSMENT FORM

WHO/WHAT

Who or what have you lost?

REMEMBER: There may be many things you will miss about the person or thing you are mourning. For example, when you lose a spouse, you also lose a best friend, your favorite cook, your biggest fan, their laughter, the one you celebrate with, etc. What will you miss most? Record thoughts, desires, questions, and complaints you have in regard to your pain.

THE EFFECT

Describe the effect of this loss on your life, both physically and spiritually. Where have you gone for help and hope? In what ways have you attempted to fix things and/or to protect yourself?

WHAT TEMPTATIONS HAVE COME FROM MY SUFFERING?

You may be tempted to let your grief affect your feelings toward God, others, and yourself. It may also result in fear, anxiety, or denial. The following examples can help you complete your assessment form.

TOWARD GOD

Doubt: I have been tempted to doubt God's character as it is revealed in Scripture (for example, "God is not good. If He were good, I would not hurt the way I am").

Anger: I have been tempted to blame God for what has happened (for example, "If He is sovereign, He could have prevented this suffering").

TOWARD OTHERS

Envy: I have been tempted to be envious and jealous of others who have not gone through the same suffering (I envy those who have been blessed in the way I want to be blessed).

Anger: I have been tempted to be angry with others (I am angry when others let me down, say the wrong thing. or forget about my pain).

TOWARD YOURSELF

Self-pity: I have been tempted to feel sorry for myself and have feelings of despair (for example, "Everyone always abandons me. I must be unworthy. I am hopeless").

Isolation: I have been tempted to isolate myself instead of reaching out to others (for example, "I am all alone").

Guilt: I have been tempted to blame myself for something that was out of my control (for example, "If I had been living a more selfless, obedient lifestyle, God would have given me children").

FEAR AND ANXIETY

In my grief I have become fearful and anxious about various things in my life, such as finances, companionship, and safety.

DENIAL

I know there are things I need to think about and emotions I should feel to truly move toward healing, but I would rather be numb and not think about them.

STOP: You will complete the "Exact nature of my wrongs" section with your mentor.

GRIEF ASSESSMENT FORM

I have said these things to you, that in me you may have peace. In the world you will have tribulation. But take heart; I have overcome the world. **JOHN 16:33**

Who/What	Remember	Effect

What temptations have come from my suffering?									Exact nature of my wrongs, faults, and mistakes (to complete with mentor)					
Toward God		Toward Others												
Doubt	Anger	Envy	Anger	Self-pity	Isolation	Guilt	Fear/anxiety	Denial	Self-centered	Self-seeking	Frightened	Dishonest	Inconsiderate	Other

PRAYER PROMPT

Fear

After you complete your assessment, confessing to God and to your mentor, walk through the prayer below. You may pray the prayer as written or use the elements of the prayer in your own words.

NOTE: Pray through each item, person, or circumstance in the assessment.

PRAYER FOR FEAR

Heavenly Father, forgive me for walking in the fear of _____. I pray that You will help me trust You more. I acknowledge that when I fear, I cannot walk in love. I realize that self-preservation is at the root of my fears. In my pride I attempt to control my world and fail to trust in Your ability to preserve my life. I forget that You are a good God and are fully in control. Therefore, today I turn these fears over to You. I trust that You will meet all my needs as You promise, not always the way I want. I trust that the ups and downs of life have purpose and that through it all, You, Lord, never change. Thank You that You are always with me. In areas of my life where I have lived under the curse of fear, I pray that You will allow me the blessing of faith that comes through grace. In Jesus' name, amen.

ELEMENTS OF THIS PRAYER
- Ask for forgiveness.
- Confess fear.
- Ask for help in trusting God.
- Acknowledge your inability to walk in love when you fear.
- Acknowledge the roots of fears.
- Turn fears over to God.
- Place your trust in God and His goodness.
- Thank God for always being with you.
- Pray for blessings of faith in areas of your life where you have walked under the curse of fear.

Grief

After you complete your assessment, confessing to God and to your mentor, walk through the prayer below. You may pray the prayer as written or use the elements of the prayer in your own words.

NOTE: Pray through each item, person, or circumstance in the assessment.

PRAYER FOR GRIEF

Father, I thank You that You are a God who hears my cries and wipes away my tears. My heart is weary and often wants to give in to despair. Give me strength and grace to believe the truth of Your character and Your Word. Increase my faith to believe that Your glory is worth this momentary affliction. Forgive me for times when I want my pain to disappear more than I want to draw near to You, even when I know You are the only One who can comfort me. I know You are the only One who can heal my broken heart and bind my wounds. Jesus, I trust You with my heart and my life because I believe in Your great love for me. Will You meet me here and walk me through this process of healing as I begin to let _____ go? Help me keep my eyes on You and Your eternal promises. [Pray and lament as you need to.] In Jesus' name, amen.

ELEMENTS OF THIS PRAYER
- Admit sorrow, hurt, grief, and pain.
- Thank God for His presence.
- Confess your tendency to seek comfort from the world rather than God.
- Acknowledge the Holy Spirit's ability to bring comfort.
- Trust God with your broken heart.
- Ask for healing.
- Ask for help.

Going Deeper

1. What makes you anxious? What do you worry about? Be specific.

> The Lord is at hand; do not be anxious about anything,
> but in everything by prayer and supplication with
> thanksgiving let your requests be made known to God.
> **PHILIPPIANS 4:5-6**

READ MATTHEW 6:19-34.

2. According to verse 19, what is easily threatened? How did Jesus instruct us, based on this reality?

3. What gospel pursuit did Jesus give us in verse 20? In what gospel truth is this rooted (see v. 21)?

4. Why might our body be full of darkness if our eye is set on earthly treasures?

> Seek first the kingdom of God and his righteousness,
> and all these things will be added to you.
> **MATTHEW 6:33**

5. What does the location of our treasure reveal about our hearts?

> The kingdom of heaven is like treasure hidden in a field,
> which a man found and covered up. Then in his joy
> he goes and sells all that he has and buys that field.
> **MATTHEW 13:44**

6. In Matthew 6:24 what does Jesus' use of the word *masters* communicate about our treasure? What verbs did He use? What was Jesus saying about how many things can rule our hearts at once?

POINT OF INTEREST: If our treasure is in heaven, our need for earthly, temporary things decreases. If our treasure is on earth, we will rail against heaven when what is most important to us is threatened.

7. Jesus began verse 25 with the word *therefore,* connecting His words with the preceding verses. How is the symptom of anxiety connected to what we treasure?

8. What command did Jesus give in verse 25? In what gospel truth did He root this command (see vv. 26-27)?

9. How did Jesus appeal to reason in verse 27?

10. How did Jesus connect anxiety and unbelief? How does faith in the gospel help resolve anxiety?

11. If anxiety reveals that our hearts are treasuring earthly, temporal things, what should our response of faith be when we recognize that our love, service, and devotion belong to something or someone other than God?

12. What gospel pursuit did Jesus give in verse 33? In what gospel truths is it rooted?

13. How will God clothe His children when His kingdom comes here on earth as it is in heaven?

GETTING TO THE ROOTS: OFFERING AND ASKING

Viewer Guide 8

COMPLETE THIS VIEWER GUIDE AS YOU WATCH THE VIDEO FOR SESSION 8.

Fruit in our life—good or bad—is really the outgrowth of what we _____, what we _____, and what we give our _____ to.

The original lie: You can go around God and not to God for _____, for validation, and for meaning—for your life to be significant.

Spiritual adultery: giving the intimacy and worship that were created for _____ to things and people

The Lord has given all of us good _____.

God does not want our desires to _____ us, and He does not owe us the fulfillment of our desires on our own terms.

THREE ENEMIES
1. The _____
2. The _____
3. The _____ realm

Satan wants to draw your attention away from God and to make you self-_____ just like he is.

Satan is always going to pounce on your _____.

Jesus shows us what it means to _____ _____ when our desires are not being met.

God can break us by His grace from the curse of our self-absorption and the bad _____ that's come with it.

The battle of your life is to continue to _____ those old ways, to _____ by His grace, and to _____ in the kingdom of God.

The Elevation of Desire

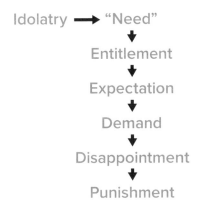

Idolatry ➡ "Need"
↓
Entitlement
↓
Expectation
↓
Demand
↓
Disappointment
↓
Punishment

Adapted from Paul David Tripp, *War of Words: Getting to the Heart of Your Communication Struggles* (Phillipsburg, NJ: P&R Publishing, 2000), 59.

Getting to the Roots of Ungodly Fruit and Character Defects

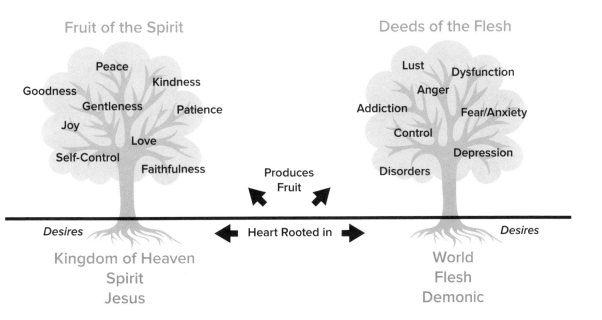

Fruit of the Spirit

Peace
Kindness
Goodness
Gentleness
Patience
Joy
Love
Self-Control
Faithfulness

Deeds of the Flesh

Lust
Dysfunction
Anger
Addiction
Fear/Anxiety
Control
Depression
Disorders

Produces Fruit

Desires ⬅ Heart Rooted in ➡ *Desires*

Kingdom of Heaven
Spirit
Jesus

World
Flesh
Demonic

DAY 1

Causes of Quarrels and Conflicts

Inordinate desires commonly produce irregular endeavors.[1]
MATTHEW HENRY

READ JAMES 4:1-10.

1. What is at the heart of fighting and conflict?

2. What does our unrighteous anger reveal?

3. At the end of verse 2, what did James suggest is part of the problem?

4. According to verse 3, what hinders our prayers?

5. According to verse 4, how does God view us when we go to the world to meet our "needs" or the things that only He can provide?

6. What does verse 5 say about God's attitude toward our hearts, affections, and worship?

7. What hope do we find in verse 6? Contrast the way God relates to the humble and the proud.

8. In light of God's grace, what are we instructed to do in verse 7?

9. Contrast the outcome of the humble with that of the proud.

1. Matthew Henry, as quoted in Tryon Edwards, *A Dictionary of Thoughts* (Detroit, MI: F. B. Dickerson, 1908), 112.

How the Battle Is Fought

READ EPHESIANS 6:10-20.

1. Where do we find the strength to be strong and stand? How powerful is "the strength of his might" (v. 10)?

> He disarmed the rulers and authorities and put them
> to open shame, by triumphing over them in him.
> **COLOSSIANS 2:15**

2. What are we instructed to do (see Eph. 6:11)? Why?

3. Ephesians 6:12 states that we are engaged in spiritual warfare. Whom do we battle?

4. The imagery of this passage describes a soldier dressed for battle. Why is it important for believers to put on the full armor of God as we engage in daily warfare?

5. What makes up the armor of God in verses 14-17? How might each piece of armor help us stand firm?

Piece of Armor	Help for Standing Firm
Belt of truth	Recognize the Enemy's lies.

6. Verses 18-20 offer instruction on prayer. When, how, and for whom do we pray?

DAY 3

Offering Ourselves as Living Sacrifices

READ ROMANS 11:33–12:8.

1. How did Paul respond to the revelation of God's wisdom and knowledge in bringing about our redemption in Christ?

2. Compare Romans 11:34 with 1 Corinthians 2:16. What additional insight do you get from the latter passage?

3. Compare Romans 11:35 with Job 41:11. What additional insight do you get from the latter passage?

4. How did Paul restate these ideas in Romans 11:36? What is the main point?

5. Chapter 12 begins with an appeal based on gospel truths. What is the basis of Paul's appeal? What was he exhorting believers to do?

6. What did Paul tell us not to do in verse 2? What did he tell us to do? Why?

7. In offering ourselves to God, we are to be used as instruments for His redemptive purposes. Describe how God intends for us to function, according to verses 3-8.

Jesus' Example in Asking

READ MATTHEW 6:9-13.

1. To whom did Jesus instruct us to pray in verse 9? Where is He located? What are we to ask Him for?

2. What did Jesus tell us to ask for in verse 10? Whose kingdom and will must we abandon?

3. In verse 11 what did Jesus tell us to ask for? In the context of the preceding verses, how does this type of praying differ from the selfish prayers that James 4:3 describes?

> You ask and do not receive, because you ask
> wrongly, to spend it on your passions.
> **JAMES 4:3**

4. What did Jesus tell us to ask for in Matthew 6:12? What expectation did Christ imply is necessary to receive forgiveness?

> If you forgive others their trespasses, your heavenly Father
> will also forgive you, but if you do not forgive others their
> trespasses, neither will your Father forgive your trespasses.
> **MATTHEW 6:14-15**

5. What did Jesus tell us to ask for in verse 13? Why can it be important to have a posture of submission before coming to the Lord in prayer with your requests?

POINT OF INTEREST: In his sermon "Our Deepest Prayer" John Piper notes that there are six petitions in these verses. The first three are about God's name, God's kingdom, and God's will. The last three are about our provision of daily bread, forgiveness of our trespasses and deliverance from evil. He concludes that the last three serve the first three in that God's name is glorified in His giving of these things.[1]

READ MATTHEW 7:7-11.

6. What are the gospel pursuits in verse 7?

7. What are the gospel promises? What are the conditions to these promises?

8. Who is inviting us to ask, seek, and knock?

> Jesus answered her, "If you knew the gift of God, and who
> it is that is saying to you, 'Give me a drink,' you would have
> asked him, and he would have given you living water."
> **JOHN 4:10**

9. What example did Jesus give to provide context for the preceding instructions?

10. In what gospel truths are these pursuits rooted?

---

1. John Piper, "Our Deepest Prayer: Hallowed Be Your Name," *desiringGod* [online], 9 January 2011 [cited 28 September 2015]. Available from the Internet: *www.desiringgod.org/messages/our-deepest-prayer-hallowed-be-your-name*.

DAY 5

Jesus' Authority

When Jesus finished these sayings, the crowds were astonished at his teaching, for he was teaching them as one who had authority, and not as their scribes.
MATTHEW 7:28-29

READ MATTHEW 8:1–10:1.

1. Who approached Jesus in Matthew 8:2? How did he approach Him? What happened?

2. Usually, what is unclean defiles and makes unclean anyone who comes in contact with that person or object. How did Jesus reverse this pattern when He touched the leper?

3. Who was the centurion? How did the centurion's authority inform the way we understand his actions? Why did Jesus marvel at him?

4. How and over what did Jesus demonstrate His authority in Matthew 8:14-17? In 8:23-27? In 8:28-34?

5. What is the cost of following Jesus, according to Matthew 8:18-22?

6. In Matthew 9:1-8 Jesus showed His authority not only to heal a paralyzed man but also to do what?

7. As the religious elite criticized Jesus for associating with sinners, how did Jesus challenge their righteousness in answering their question about fasting?

8. Describe the scene when Jesus restored life to a ruler's daughter.

9. Describe the scene when Jesus healed the woman suffering from the discharge of blood.

10. Describe the scene when Jesus healed two blind men.

11. Describe the scene when Jesus healed a mute man.

12. What did Jesus say and do in 9:37 and 10:1?

God Is Jealous for Our Hearts

READ LUKE 18:18-30.

1. What did the rich ruler call Jesus?

> He asked them, "But who do you say that I am?"
> Peter answered him, "You are the Christ."
> **MARK 8:29**

2. How did Jesus respond to him? How did Jesus reveal the truth about who He was?

3. How did the rich man answer? What misunderstanding made him respond this way?

4. What was Jesus addressing in the rich ruler's heart?

> Where your treasure is, there your heart will be also.
> **MATTHEW 6:21**

5. Why do you think it is easier for a camel to go through the eye of a needle than for a rich person to enter the kingdom of God?

6. What gospel truth did Jesus proclaim to give hope (see Luke 18:27)?

7. How did Jesus highlight the First and Second Commandments and the first part of the Great Commandment?

> You say, I am rich, I have prospered, and I need nothing, not
> realizing that you are wretched, pitiable, poor, blind, and naked.
> **REVELATION 3:17**

8. What is the cost of following Jesus? What is the value of giving up things in this life for the sake of the kingdom?

Going Deeper

1. Internal ruling desires lead to fights and quarrels. What desires tend to rule your heart and spark anger?

2. What do you turn to instead of God to fulfill your desires?

3. How do you attempt to satisfy your desire for peace?

4. Where do you typically look for hope?

5. Where do you find value, worth, and significance?

> Far be it from me to boast except in the cross of our Lord Jesus Christ, by which the world has been crucified to me, and I to the world.
> **GALATIANS 6:14**

6. We all have an innate desire to belong to something bigger than ourselves. Historically, what lengths have you gone to in order to belong? Today what do you have in common with those who are closest to you?

7. To what lengths have you gone to meet your material needs? Have you ever sinned to meet those needs?

> My God will supply every need of yours according to his riches in glory in Christ Jesus. To our God and Father be glory forever and ever. Amen.
> **PHILIPPIANS 4:19-20**

8. When we withhold an area of our lives from Christ and His lordship (authority), to whom do we give authority by default?

9. What character defects do you need to surrender to Jesus, trusting Him to provide the grace you need?

10. Are there areas of your life in which you still feel enslaved?

11. Are there physical, emotional, spiritual, or relational wounds that you desire Jesus to heal?

12. What gospel truths and gospel pursuits affected you most this week?

STEP 6: We are entirely ready to have God remove all these defects of character.

> Restore to me the joy of your salvation,
> and uphold me with a willing spirit.
> **PSALM 51:12**

STEP 7: We humbly asked Him to remove our shortcomings.

> Which one of you, if his son asks him for bread, will give him a stone?
> Or if he asks for a fish, will give him a serpent? If you then, who are
> evil, know how to give good gifts to your children, how much more will
> your Father who is in heaven give good things to those who ask him!
> **MATTHEW 7:9-11**

REDEEMED TRUTH FROM STEPS 6 & 7: In attempting to live independent of God, we have developed dysfunctional (sinful) patterns of coping. After careful examination we have begun to see the demonic roots of our slavery to these sinful patterns. We desire freedom. We renounce our former ways; offer ourselves to God; and, under the waterfall of His grace, ask Him to deliver and heal us by the authority of Christ and the power of the Holy Spirit. We also pray for blessing and the empowerment of the Holy Spirit to live life according to His kingdom purposes.

> Truly, I say to you, whoever says to this mountain, "Be taken up and thrown
> into the sea," and does not doubt in his heart, but believes that what he
> says will come to pass, it will be done for him. Therefore I tell you, whatever
> you ask in prayer, believe that you have received it, and it will be yours.
> **MARK 11:23-24**

PEACEMAKING, PART 1: RECONCILING AND AMENDING

Viewer Guide 9

COMPLETE THIS VIEWER GUIDE AS YOU WATCH THE VIDEO FOR SESSION 9.

The way we engage horizontally with others is informed by what takes place _____.

In making amends, we have to make sure that we _____ rightly.

Idols confuse, skew our vision to see rightly, and _____ us from God.

What makes an idol bad is the way it provides comfort or peace or identity that is not derived from _____.

If we don't see rightly, we'll never _____.

If we're known to God, we don't have to justify ourselves. We don't have to posture. We don't have to go in _____.

Every sin that you've committed—your history—is _____ when Christ invades your life.

If you have sinned against someone, _____.

We confess, regardless of the _____.

We go _____ with the aim to please Christ.

PRINCIPLES OF PEACEMAKING

1. _____ specific attitudes and actions.

2. _____ the hurt and express regret for all of the harm done.

3. Accompanied by altered attitudes and actions, _____ and change in repentance.

NOTES

DAY 1

Dealing with Our Own Hearts First

The heart is deceitful above all things,
   and desperately sick;
   who can understand it?
JEREMIAH 17:9

READ EZEKIEL 14:1-8.

1. The elders of Israel came before the prophet Ezekiel to ask of the Lord. What did the Lord want to talk to them about first?

2. Why did God want to talk to the elders about these things, according to verse 5?

3. How did the Lord instruct us to deal with our idols?

4. What is God most concerned about?

5. Consider the imagery. How well will we be able to see if a stumbling block of sin hinders our vision? What do you think we will see?

6. How does our idolatry cloud our judgment?

MEDITATE ON THE FOLLOWING VERSE.

You hypocrite, first take the log out of your own eye, and then
you will see clearly to take the speck out of your brother's eye.
MATTHEW 7:5

Ministry of Reconciliation

READ 2 CORINTHIANS 5:11-21.

1. What understanding leads believers to persuade others (see v. 11)?

> We must all appear before the judgment seat of Christ, so that each one may
> receive what is due for what he has done in the body, whether good or evil.
> **2 CORINTHIANS 5:10**

2. Where does a believer's security come from?

3. Why did Paul talk about the fact that he had clean motives and a pure heart?

> The LORD said to Samuel, "Do not look on his appearance or on the height of
> his stature, because I have rejected him. For the LORD sees not as man sees:
> man looks on the outward appearance, but the LORD looks on the heart."
> **1 SAMUEL 16:7**

4. If Paul and Timothy's actions seemed foolish, for whom were they intended
    (see 2 Cor. 5:13)? If they seemed right, whom were they for?

182

Since, in the wisdom of God, the world did not know God through wisdom, it
pleased God through the folly of what we preach to save those who believe.
1 CORINTHIANS 1:21

5. What was Paul and Timothy's compelling motivation (see 2 Cor. 5:14)?

If I speak in the tongues of men and of angels, but have
not love, I am a noisy gong or a clanging cymbal.
1 CORINTHIANS 13:1

6. How does 2 Corinthians 5:11-21 explain Paul and Timothy's apparent lack
of self-concern?

7. Because Christ died for all believers, for whom are we to live (see v. 15)?

Whoever loves his life loses it, and whoever hates
his life in this world will keep it for eternal life.
JOHN 12:25

8. According to 2 Corinthians 5:17, how does God describe those who are
in Christ? What is significant about these words?

He who was seated on the throne said, "Behold, I am making all things new."
Also he said, "Write this down, for these words are trustworthy and true."
REVELATION 21:5

9. According to 2 Corinthians 5:18, what is also true about those who are in Christ? What is our ministry?

10. With what message have we been entrusted? What does the message contain? For whom are we messengers?

11. What does it mean to be an ambassador? As ambassadors, what are we calling others to do (see v. 20)?

> "Yet even now," declares the LORD,
>   "return to me with all your heart,
>   with fasting, with weeping, and with mourning;
>   and rend your hearts and not your garments."
>   Return to the LORD your God,
>   for he is gracious and merciful,
>   slow to anger, and abounding in steadfast love;
>   and he relents over disaster.
> **JOEL 2:12-13**

> Nothing can save us but the restoration of our lost humility,
> the original and only true relationship of the creature to its God.[1]
> **ANDREW MURRAY**

---

1. Andrew Murray, *Humility: The Journey Toward Holiness* (Bloomington, MN: Bethany House, 2001), 16.

DAY 3

Motivation of Love

READ 1 CORINTHIANS 13.

1. Verses 1-3 list a large number of gifts and talents. Even if we have all these gifts and talents, what are we without love?

2. What are some aspects of love described in verses 4-7?

3. What will never end? What will end?

4. As we mature, what will we give up?

> He died for all, that those who live might no longer live for
> themselves but for him who for their sake died and was raised.
> **2 CORINTHIANS 5:15**

5. How did Paul describe our ability to see in 1 Corinthians 13:12? What does this verse promise?

6. Which of the three Christian qualities in verse 13 is the greatest?

MEDITATE ON THE FOLLOWING VERSE.

> We love because he first loved us.
> **1 JOHN 4:19**

DAY 4

Walk in Love

READ EPHESIANS 5.

1. What instruction did Paul give in verse 1? How does a child's imitation of his or her parents reflect how we should imitate God?

2. How does Christ's example show us how to love one another?

3. What does this example not include, according to verse 3? What gospel identity do we find in these commands?

4. What did Paul say has no place among the saints? What should be among us instead?

5. How did Paul remind the Ephesians of what God has done through the gospel to lead them away from lawless behavior and toward grateful obedience?

6. What "empty words" (v. 6) do you suppose Paul was warning the church about?

7. How did Paul say we should interact with those who justify these practices?

8. Ephesians 5:14 reflects the poetic imagery of Isaiah 60. What hope do we bring as children of light?

> Arise, shine, for your light has come,
>   and the glory of the LORD has risen upon you.
> **ISAIAH 60:1**

Go and Be Reconciled

READ MATTHEW 5:23-26.

1. What should we do if we remember that someone has something against us?

2. What is the order of importance in these verses?

3. Is there a sense of urgency?

4. What does this teaching say about God's desire for unity in the church?

5. Keeping short accounts means we deal with our debts to others in a timely manner. Why do you think God calls believers to keep short accounts (see v. 25)?

> ... so as to walk in a manner worthy of the Lord, fully pleasing to him,
> bearing fruit in every good work, and increasing in the knowledge of God.
> **COLOSSIANS 1:10**

READ NUMBERS 5:5-7.

6. What general principles does this text teach us about how to respond when we realize our sin against another person?

READ LUKE 15:18-19.

7. How low was the prodigal son willing to submit himself to in order to reconcile with his father?

MEDITATE ON THE FOLLOWING VERSE.

I will arise and go to my father, and I will say to him, "Father, I have sinned against heaven and before you. I am no longer worthy to be called your son. Treat me as one of your hired servants."
LUKE 15:18-19

Making a List of Amends

Sin not only fractures our relationship with God but also affects those around us. Our sin always has collateral damage. Today we will seek God for what steps of faith and obedience to take in reconciling relationships. We have spent a great deal of time examining our hearts before the Lord. We now humble ourselves and confess our sin to those affected.

> If you are offering your gift at the altar and there remember that your brother
> has something against you, leave your gift there before the altar and go.
> First be reconciled to your brother, and then come and offer your gift.
> **MATTHEW 5:23-24**

After praying, reviewing your assessment, and talking to your mentor, to whom do you owe amends? What specifically do you need to confess, and from whom do you need to seek forgiveness? Are you willing to make amends to everyone?

> If possible, so far as it depends on you, live peaceably with all.
> **ROMANS 12:18**

Make a list of the people your sin has affected. Indicate which of these people you need to make amends with, why you need to make amends with them, and whether you are willing to do so. Order your list of needed amends by priority: (1) would be primary to make amends; (2) would be secondary; (3) need prayer, counsel, or timing; and (4) never.

To Whom?   **For What?**   **Willing (Y/N)?**   **Priority (1–4)**

Going Deeper

Whatever you wish that others would do to you, do
also to them, for this is the Law and the Prophets.
MATTHEW 7:12

1. How does fear prevent you from loving others as Christ does? Give specific examples from your life (confronting difficult situations, willingness to share your faith, etc.).

There is no fear in love, but perfect love casts out fear. For fear has to do
with punishment, and whoever fears has not been perfected in love.
1 JOHN 4:18

2. Have you ever used your knowledge and intellect as a source of pride to beat people down rather than build them up? Give examples.

"Knowledge" puffs up, but love builds up.
1 CORINTHIANS 8:1

If anyone imagines that he knows something,
he does not yet know as he ought to know.
1 CORINTHIANS 8:2

3. Describe times when your idolatry has distorted your judgment in acting according to God's will.

4. In Matthew 5:23-24 the Lord taught the importance of being reconciled prior to bringing our gifts before the altar. Describe situations in which you offended someone with whom you need to be reconciled.

5. Are there people or institutions to whom you are unwilling to confess and make restitution? Be specific.

STEP 8: We made a list of all persons we had harmed and became willing to make amends to them all.

> If possible, so far as it depends on you, live peaceably with all.
> **ROMANS 12:18**

STEP 9: We made direct amends to such people whenever possible, except when to do so would injure them or others.

> The LORD spoke to Moses, saying, "Speak to the people of Israel, When a man or woman commits any of the sins that people commit by breaking faith with the LORD, and that person realizes his guilt, he shall confess his sin that he has committed. And he shall make full restitution for his wrong, adding a fifth to it and giving it to him to whom he did the wrong."
> **NUMBERS 5:5-7**

REDEEMED TRUTH FROM STEPS 8 & 9: Relationships break down because of sin. If there were no sin in the world, relationships would work harmoniously, evidenced by love and unity. Division among God's people provides opportunities to identify sin and purify the body. The gospel of Jesus Christ brings about justice in a way that the law cannot by inwardly reconciling the very heart of injustice to God. As those forgiven by God, we can humbly approach those affected by our sin and make amends. This change of heart brings glory to God by demonstrating the power of the gospel and reflecting His heart in bringing justice through His reconciled people.

PEACEMAKING, PART 2: CONFRONTING AND FORGIVING

Viewer Guide 10

COMPLETE THIS VIEWER GUIDE AS YOU WATCH THE VIDEO FOR SESSION 10.

Is this an area of wisdom or _____, or is this sin?

What is being looked at is the hard-heartedness of being engaged and confronted by a brother who is unwilling to _____.

When you see your brother in sin, we, in love, _____.

This process of engaging reveals what is already _____.

In the process of discipline where many are gathered, it is so serious that _____ Himself is present.

We confront because _____ confronts us in our sin.

We forgive because we're _____.

It is possible for us to forgive and not _____ the facts.

There's this _____ in marriage that really requires more forgiveness and more confrontation than any other relationship.

Conflict Wheel

Biblical Peacemaking
Speaking the Truth in Love

Spirit

Avoidant Responses
(Passive/Flight)

Attack Responses
(Aggressive /Fight)

Adapted from Ken Sande, *The Peacemaker* (Grand Rapids, MI: Baker, 2004).

NOTES

_____

_____

_____

_____

_____

_____

_____

_____

_____

_____

Gospel-Centered Community Brings Unity

READ MATTHEW 18:1-20.

1. We see conflict among the disciples in verse 1. What were they arguing about?

2. How did Jesus intervene to resolve the conflict?

> Where jealousy and selfish ambition exist,
> there will be disorder and every vile practice.
> **JAMES 3:16**

3. How did the example of becoming like children give the disciples insight into how they must enter the kingdom of heaven? What virtue is the basis for greatness in the kingdom of heaven? How does a child demonstrate this characteristic?

> Blessed are the poor in spirit, for theirs is the kingdom of heaven.
> **MATTHEW 5:3**

4. According to Matthew 18:5,10, how should Christ's covenant community respond to those seeking help and direction in their weaknesses? What characteristics of God's heart are exemplified?

5. What awaits those who mislead or take advantage of others in their weakness? How do these verses show us the virtue of justice?

6. What warning does verse 7 give to the world? How does gospel-centered community contrast in the way it deals with sin?

7. Rather than despising "these little ones" (v. 10), what are we to do if they go astray (see vv. 10-14)?

8. Our pursuits reveal the things we love. How does the covenant community's pursuit of a straying sheep reveal God's heart? What does a church's neglect of pursuit indicate?

9. Who watches over the sheep when it strays?

10. What takes place when the stray sheep is found?

11. Who do we understand the sheep to be?

12. What loving steps of Christian accountability did Jesus outline to address someone who sins against you (see vv. 15-16)?

13. If the person does not listen, what steps should the church take to discipline him or her?

14. Many churches do not practice church discipline, saying it is unloving, and celebrate themselves as a place of grace and tolerance. How could you use this Scripture passage to make a defense that neglecting church discipline is a misunderstanding of love and grace?

You are arrogant! Ought you not rather to mourn?
Let him who has done this be removed from among you.
1 CORINTHIANS 5:2

Forgiveness

READ MATTHEW 18:21-35.

1. What do you think this parable intends to remind us of when confronting a brother or a sister in sin?

2. Peter apparently believed he was being very gracious in the question he asked Jesus. How did Jesus respond?

3. What parable did Jesus use to describe the kingdom of heaven? What was the situation (see v. 23)?

4. How much did the first servant owe his master? What would that amount equate to today? What did the law require?

5. What did the first servant offer to do? Was his offer realistic?

6. How did his master respond?

7. What did the first servant do to the second servant?

8. How much did the second servant owe the first servant? What would that amount equate to today?

9. What did the second servant offer to do?

10. How did the first servant respond? What did his reaction reveal about his heart?

11. How did the fellow servants respond?

12. How did the master deal with the first servant?

13. What lesson was Jesus teaching (see v. 35)?

MEDITATE ON THE FOLLOWING VERSES.

If you forgive others their trespasses, your heavenly Father
will also forgive you, but if you do not forgive others their
trespasses, neither will your Father forgive your trespasses.
MATTHEW 6:14-15

More on Confronting and Forgiving

READ LUKE 17:1-10.

1. How likely is it that you will encounter "temptations to sin," according to verse 1?

2. How do Jesus' words in verse 2 assure us of God's justice?

3. What are you instructed to do if your brother sins, according to verse 3? If he repents, what should you do?

4. What must you do if your brother sins against you and repents seven times in a day?

5. Can you identify with the disciples' response in verse 5?

6. Jesus told the disciples that obedience in forgiving requires faith the size of a mustard seed. If increased faith is not the issue, what is the issue?

7. In verses 7-10 Jesus told the story of the unworthy servants to support His point. How do you think the servants felt at the end of a long day plowing in the fields?

8. What were the servants not asked to do? What were they asked to do?

9. How much did their obedience have to do with feelings and emotions?

10. How much did Jesus' command to forgive have to do with the way we feel?

MEDITATE ON THE FOLLOWING VERSES.

You shall not hate your brother in your heart, but you shall reason frankly with your neighbor, lest you incur sin because of him. You shall not take vengeance or bear a grudge against the sons of your own people, but you shall love your neighbor as yourself: I am the LORD.
LEVITICUS 19:17-18

Ministry of Reconciliation: Example from the Scriptures

READ PHILEMON.

1. Who was the author of Philemon? Where was he when he wrote the letter? To whom did he write? Where did the church meet? Who is the subject of this letter?

2. What did Paul extend to Philemon in verse 3? How might this greeting help shape Paul's hopes for Onesimus?

3. Why was Paul grateful to God for Philemon?

4. We see that Paul's prayers preceded his petition of Philemon. In what ways would Paul's prayer be answered if reconciliation occurred? For whose name's sake did he pray?

5. How did Paul appeal to Philemon? Based on his authority, could he have approached him differently?

6. What gospel fruit did Paul testify to as he made his appeal to Philemon for Onesimus?

7. How did Paul expect the remarkable change in Onesimus to affect the way Philemon related to him?

8. What would be required of Philemon for the relationship to be reconciled?

9. Who was the minister of reconciliation in this letter? Who was the offending party? Who was the offended party? Who or what was the means of grace that would allow these parties to be reconciled in their hearts?

10. It appears that Onesimus himself would have carried this letter back to Philemon. What possible consequences may have awaited him? What does that possibility say about Onesimus?

Ambassadors Appealing to the Lost

We have been entrusted with the ministry of reconciliation, imploring those outside the Kingdom to be reconciled to God and pointing them to the cross, where they can receive God's grace.

Imagine a person who suffered abuse at the hands of another. Healed by the resurrecting power of Jesus Christ, they go to their abuser and demonstrate love by pointing them toward new life through the cross of Christ. That action would truly be a picture of Christ! That is the ministry of reconciliation.

READ JONAH.

1. What did God ask of Jonah?

2. What was Jonah's response? What is the correlation between God's presence and Jonah's disobedience?

> Where shall I go from your Spirit?
> Or where shall I flee from your presence?
> **PSALM 139:7**

3. Research the direction and distance of Tarshish to Nineveh. What did you find?

4. How did God intervene in response to Jonah's rebellion?

5. What is evident from Jonah's prayer while inside the fish?

6. What did God ask of Jonah at the beginning of chapter 3? Does His directive sound familiar?

7. How did Jonah respond?

8. How did the people of Nineveh respond? How did God respond to them?

9. We might expect the story to end after chapter 3. Whom did God continue to engage in chapter 4?

10. Research the history of the Ninevites in relation to the nation of Israel. Why might Jonah personally have been reluctant to go to Nineveh?

11. What do we learn about God's heart toward the Ninevites?

12. What does God's pursuit of Jonah's heart say about God's desire for the hearts of His people?

Unity in the Body of Christ

READ EPHESIANS 4:1-16.

1. What was Paul calling the church in Ephesus to pursue?

2. How do verses 2-3 describe this "walk"?

3. How did Paul, in his repetitive use of the word *one,* remind us of what unifies believers in Christ?

4. What is true for every believer, according to verse 7?

5. What specific roles does Christ give to the church for equipping the saints (see v. 11)?

6. What are these roles to equip the saints to do? Until when? Why?

7. How does verse 14 describe children?

8. How does verse 15 describe a mature person?

9. What does a functional church body require? What is the result?

Going Deeper

1. As people repent and confess sin to us, we need to be ready to offer forgiveness. Our forgiveness is evidence that Christ's forgiveness has transformed our hearts and that we want them to be reconciled to God. Prayerfully consider and list the names of people whom you might have difficulty forgiving.

> Just so, I tell you, there will be more joy in heaven over one sinner who repents than over ninety-nine righteous persons who need no repentance.
> **LUKE 15:7**

2. Are there brothers or sisters in Christ who may have sinned against you and continue to walk in significant unrepentant sin? Prayerfully consider how God is calling you to forgive these people for the sin they committed against you.

> Brothers, if anyone is caught in any transgression, you who are spiritual should restore him in a spirit of gentleness. Keep watch on yourself, lest you too be tempted.
> **GALATIANS 6:1**

3. Now that bitterness, fear, and shame no longer rule you, are there people outside the body of Christ who may have hurt you and need to be offered peace with God through the blood of Christ?

4. Where are you stuck? Discuss with your group any situations in which you are unwilling to make amends, forgive, confront, or share the gospel. Why?

5. Discuss any fears you have in making amends, forgiving, confronting someone's sin, or sharing the hope of the gospel. Why are you afraid?

6. Are there any relationships you believe are beyond repair?

7. Spend time in prayer as a group, specifically for those situations.

8. Discuss any other questions or issues you are facing.

ADDITIONAL REDEEMED TRUTH FROM STEPS 8 & 9: As ambassadors of Christ, we are to be instruments of grace as we confront those who sin against us. We hand our offenses over to God and extend eager forgiveness to those who ask for it. And in this way, fellowship with God and among His people is preserved.

PERSEVERING AND PURSUING

Viewer Guide 11

COMPLETE THIS VIEWER GUIDE AS YOU WATCH THE VIDEO FOR SESSION 11.

The gospel is continuing to create _____ and _____ within us to continue.

Joy: deep, overwhelming, even painful _____ and yearning for something near yet unattained, tinged with unwavering _____

Joy is the result of our pursuit of _____.

_____ with Christ is the foundation of our joy.

UNION WITH CHRIST

1. We're growing in increasing _____ to Christ.
2. It shapes how we see the world and pursue _____.

   Christ becomes my _____.

SPIRITUAL DISCIPLINES

- The _____ of God
- _____
- _____

- _____
- _____

3. We _____ with a sense of an enduring joy.

   The _____ is at work to help you persevere.

PERSEVERING THROUGH SUFFERING

1. We must _____ our understanding of suffering and trials.
2. We must see that persevering through suffering is an element that is found in _____.

There's this understanding of persevering that I can endure the loss of things, the trial of things, the pain of things, that I might be able to _____ Him better.

In persevering, for the believer, there is a _____ that comes in knowing and pursuing Him.

Pursuing Treasure

Position
Physique
Power
People
Personality
Prosperity
Possessions
Posterity

Christ

Posterity
Possessions
Prosperity
Personality
People
Power
Physique
Position

Dependence/Slavery

Stewardship/Freedom

NOTES

Looking to Jesus in Our Difficulties

READ HEBREWS 12:1-17.

1. To what action are we called (see v. 1)?

> We have come to share in Christ, if indeed we hold
> our original confidence firm to the end.
> **HEBREWS 3:14**

2. Why do you think both weight and sin are mentioned in Hebrews 12:1? Do you think they are the same or different?

3. To whom do we look? How is He described?

4. What did He do and why? What was the result?

5. What does it mean that He despised the shame? What does it mean to despise something?

Count it all joy, my brothers, when you meet trials of various
kinds, for you know that the testing of your faith produces
steadfastness. And let steadfastness have its full effect,
that you may be perfect and complete, lacking in nothing.
JAMES 1:2-4

6. Why should we consider Jesus and what He suffered (see Heb. 12:3)?

A disciple is not above his teacher, nor a servant above his master.
MATTHEW 10:24

7. What is true about the person whom the Lord disciplines (see Heb. 12:5-13)?
Why does the Lord discipline?

8. What should we strive for, according to verse 14?

READ JAMES 1:2-18.

9. How did James indicate we should view trials in our lives?

10. What is the purpose of our trials, and what is the result?

11. If we lack wisdom amid trials, what are we instructed to do? Why?

12. How should we view worldly wealth and perishing enjoyments?

13. What person will be blessed amid suffering? What will he or she receive?

MEDITATE ON THE FOLLOWING VERSE.

You have need of endurance, so that when you have done
the will of God you may receive what is promised.
HEBREWS 10:36

DAY 2

The Surpassing Worth of Knowing Christ

> The kingdom of heaven is like treasure hidden in a field,
> which a man found and covered up. Then in his joy
> he goes and sells all that he has and buys that field.
> **MATTHEW 13:44**

READ PHILIPPIANS 3.

1. What warning did Paul give in verse 2?

2. How did Paul describe the true circumcision?

3. Where do people who are not of the true circumcision derive
    their confidence? On what do they base their righteousness?

4. What reasons could Paul give for having confidence in the flesh?

5. What did he count those things? What did he count everything?

6. Why did Paul count those things as loss and rubbish?

7. For what was Paul willing to forsake his flesh?

8. How did Paul view suffering and hardship?

9. Summarize Paul's words in verses 12-16.

10. What warning did Paul give in verses 17-21? Contrast believers and the enemies of the cross in this passage. Identify their pursuits and the corresponding results.

> Not everyone who says to me, "Lord, Lord", will enter the kingdom of heaven, but the one who does the will of my Father who is in heaven. On that day many will say to me, "Lord, Lord, did we not prophesy in your name, and cast out demons in your name, and do many mighty works in your name?" And then will I declare to them, "I never knew you; depart from me, you workers of lawlessness."
> **MATTHEW 7:21-23**

Training and Disciplines

People do not drift toward holiness. Apart from grace-driven effort, people do not gravitate toward godliness, prayer, obedience to Scripture, faith, and delight in the Lord. We drift toward compromise and call it tolerance; we drift toward disobedience and call it freedom; we drift toward superstition and call it faith. We cherish the indiscipline of lost self-control and call it relaxation; we slouch toward prayerlessness and delude ourselves into thinking we have escaped legalism; we slide toward godlessness and convince ourselves we have been liberated.[1]

D. A. CARSON

READ 1 CORINTHIANS 9:24-27.

1. What do these verses compare our lives to?

2. Compare and contrast the prize we seek in our Christian walk versus the prize awarded after a competitive race.

3. How do these verses instruct us to run?

4. Compare and contrast training in godliness and physical training.

> While bodily training is of some value, godliness is of value in every way,
> as it holds promise for the present life and also for the life to come.
> **1 TIMOTHY 4:8**

5. What happens if you stop caring for your physical body? How does the picture these verses provide give you insight into spiritual disciplines?

> ... that I may know him and the power of his resurrection, and may
> share his sufferings, becoming like him in his death, that by any
> means possible I may attain the resurrection from the dead.
> **PHILIPPIANS 3:10-11**

6. According to 1 Corinthians 9:27, what may happen if you are not in good shape spiritually?

> Seek first the kingdom of God and his righteousness,
> and all these things will be added to you.
> **MATTHEW 6:33**

READ MATTHEW 6:1-18.

7. What warning did Jesus give in verse 1 about acts of righteousness?

8. What do hypocrites do? Why do they do it? What is their reward?

9. What should we do? What will be our reward?

> Beware of practicing your righteousness before
> other people in order to be seen by them, for then you
> will have no reward from your Father who is in heaven.
> **MATTHEW 6:1**

10. What warning did Jesus give about the mindless repetition of the Gentiles (see v. 7)?

11. What should we do instead?

12. When you fast, what should you not do? What should you do?

1. D. A. Carson, "For the Love of God," 23 January 2014 [cited 6 August 2015]. Available from the Internet: *www.thegospelcoalition.org*.

Filling a Thirsty Soul

READ PSALM 63.

1. Where was David when he wrote this song? How does verse 1 describe this land?

2. According to verse 1, where did David turn to quench his thirst during these difficult circumstances? How would you describe his pursuit? What does this reveal about his heart?

3. How does Psalm 63 demonstrate worship?

4. How confident was David that he would be satisfied and would praise God?

5. Who was the source of his confidence? Why?

6. What did David consider better than life?

7. What did David believe he would find in his pursuits?

8. According to Psalm 63, when would David's soul be satisfied?

> Do not be conformed to this world, but be transformed by the renewal of your mind, that by testing you may discern what is the will of God, what is good and acceptable and perfect.
> **ROMANS 12:2**

9. In Psalm 63 what was David's soul doing as God upheld him?

10. What would happen to those who sought to destroy David's life?

READ EPHESIANS 5:15-21.

11. How do verses 15-16 call us to live?

12. How do we live this way, according to verse 18?

13. What does it mean to be filled with the Spirit?

POINT OF INTEREST: Empty, vain religion is man's attempt, by the work of his own hands, to appease a deity to get what he wants. Such religious activity stands in contrast to a lifestyle of gospel-centered worship, which is a response to everything already given to us through Christ and His redemptive work.

Walk by the Spirit

READ GALATIANS 5.

> You will know the truth, and the truth will set you free.
> **JOHN 8:32**

1. Why did Christ set us free, according to Galatians 5:1?

2. What did Paul warn the church in Galatia not to do?

In the Old Testament, circumcision was required to keep the law. Some people in the church of Galatia were trying to return to the law by implying that justification comes through faith in Christ plus adherence to certain aspects of the law. In Acts 15 we find the following passage.

> Some men came down from Judea and were teaching
> the brothers, "Unless you are circumcised according
> to the custom of Moses, you cannot be saved."
> **ACTS 15:1**

3. In Galatians 5 what did Paul say to those who wished to return to the law or, in this case, circumcision?

4. Paul said, "In Christ Jesus neither circumcision nor uncircumcision counts for anything" (v. 6). What does count?

5. If Paul still preached circumcision, what would that suggest?

> I do not nullify the grace of God, for if righteousness
> were through the law, then Christ died for no purpose.
> **GALATIANS 2:21**

6. In Galatians 5 what sentiments did Paul have toward those who tried to persuade others that justification comes through obeying the law? Why?

7. What did Paul caution the church not to do with its freedom (see v. 13)? Why (see v. 21)?

8. What will you not do if you walk by the Spirit? Why?

9. What is true if you are led by the Spirit (see v. 18)?

MEDITATE ON THE FOLLOWING VERSE.

> Do not get drunk with wine, for that is debauchery,
> but be filled with the Spirit.
> **EPHESIANS 5:18**

The Soils

READ LUKE 8:4-15.

1. Who was Jesus' audience for this parable?

2. Based on verse 10, does it appear that Jesus intended for everyone in the crowd to understand His message?

3. Who has the ability to understand, according to verse 8?

4. Describe each of the four soils on which the seed fell (see vv. 5-8).

5. What happened to the seed in each case?

6. What was Jesus' reason for teaching in parables?

7. What did Jesus reveal the seed to be?

8. How did Jesus explain the situation of the seed that fell along the path? What did this seed represent? What was the result?

9. How did Jesus explain the seed that fell among the rocks? What did this seed represent? What was the result?

10. How did Jesus explain the situation of the seed that fell among the thorns? What did this seed represent? What was the result?

11. How did Jesus explain the situation of the seed that fell on good soil? What did this seed represent? What was the result?

Be patient, therefore, brothers, until the coming of the Lord. See
how the farmer waits for the precious fruit of the earth, being
patient about it, until it receives the early and the late rains.
JAMES 5:7

Going Deeper

I have fought the good fight, I have finished the race, I have kept the faith.
2 TIMOTHY 4:7

1. What sin or weight do you need to lay aside in order to run the race well?

2. What trials are you facing in your life? In what ways are you tempted to preempt God's purposes of sanctification while under trial?

3. How do you know when you are walking by the Spirit? How does this walk express itself in your life with the people and circumstances you encounter (family, coworkers, children, prayer life, etc.)?

4. What would obedience to Christ look like in your life?

His master said to him, "Well done, good and faithful servant. You have been faithful over a little; I will set you over much. Enter into the joy of your master."
MATTHEW 25:23

5. When you are thirsting in the wilderness, where do you turn for satisfaction? What does this response reveal about your heart?

6. On what do you tend to obsess, fantasize, meditate, or dwell? Be specific. What is the result (fear, anxiety, depression, worship, praise, joy, etc.)?

7. What stirs your affection for Christ?

8. Being undisciplined leads to laziness or apathy. How disciplined are you in engaging spiritual disciplines daily? If you are undisciplined, why?

9. What does a disciplined life look like specifically for you?

10. What are your goals and motivations for living a disciplined life?

> O God, you are my God; earnestly I seek you;
>   my soul thirsts for you;
> my flesh faints for you,
>   as in a dry and weary land where there is no water.
> **PSALM 63:1**

11. Are there things you need to say no to in order to love the Lord and in turn love your spouse, family, friends, neighbors, and coworkers?

STEP 10: We continued to take personal inventory and, when we were wrong, promptly admitted it.

> If you are offering your gift at the altar and there remember that your brother
> has something against you, leave your gift there before the altar and go.
> First be reconciled to your brother, and then come and offer your gift.
> **MATTHEW 5:23-24**

STEP 11: We sought through prayer and meditation to improve our conscious contact with God, praying only for the knowledge of His will and the power to carry that out.

> ... that I may know him and the power of his resurrection,
> and may share his sufferings, becoming like him in his death.
> **PHILIPPIANS 3:10**

REDEEMED TRUTH FROM STEPS 10 & 11: We continue in the fear of the Lord, putting to death those things that rob our affections for Christ while persevering in our loving and joyful obedience to Him. We return to the Lord quickly with an attitude of repentance, when out of step with the Spirit, as we're trained in godliness and grow spiritually. Since He is our ultimate treasure, we seek to know Him and fill ourselves with those things that stir our affections for Him. We practice spiritual disciplines so that our hearts, so prone to wander, might stay in rhythm with His.

THE JOY OF MAKING MUCH OF HIS NAME

Viewer Guide 12

Joy hasn't met its completion until it's been passed on and _____.

God Himself is extending an invitation to enter into His _____.

The God of the universe is extending a personal invitation to join Him in His _____.

God is literally making His appeal through _____.

Because Jesus' authority is global, His _____ is global.

Jesus' _____ is global.

The Spirit will come upon you, and you will be My _____.

You could walk out of _____. You could walk out of the bondage of _____ that all of us were born into.

God is inviting you to take this story that He's given you—the story of _____, the story of hope, the story of a God who loves you, cares for you, and has demonstrated His love and His care for you in the sending of His Son.

This message is the greatest invitation to _____.

God is extending a generous and genuine invitation to _____ Him in His work— His work of redemption.

Comprehensive Gospel

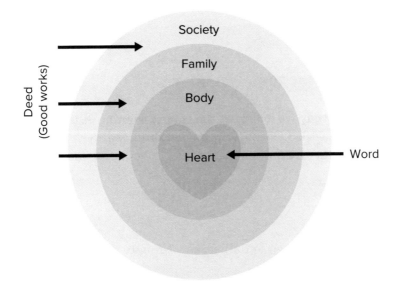

NOTES

The Great Commission

READ MATTHEW 28:16-20.

1. Earlier in the study we looked at the commissioning of the prophet Isaiah (see Isa. 6 and week 3, day 2). Why do you think Matthew 28:19-20 is referred to as the Great Commission?

2. Why did the disciples go to Galilee, according to verse 16?

3. How do they respond to Jesus' appearance?

4. What gospel truth did Jesus convey to combat doubt when He appeared to the disciples after His resurrection (see v. 18)?

5. With what gospel imperative did Christ instruct His disciples?

6. Jesus said we make disciples by teaching people to obey all His commands. How is making disciples different from just teaching them all His commands?

7. In what gospel truth did Jesus then root His disciples (see v. 20)?

READ GENESIS 12:1-3.

8. How do the verses in Matthew 28 echo God's call of Abram?

9. According to Genesis 12:2, for what purpose was Abram blessed and raised up? Whom was Abram's blessing to bless, according to verse 3?

10. Reread Ephesians 2:1-10. This passage describes what the gospel has accomplished for every believer. What is God displaying (see v. 7)? According to verse 10, why has God created us in Christ Jesus?

MEDITATE ON THE FOLLOWING VERSE.

We are his workmanship, created in Christ Jesus for good works,
which God prepared beforehand, that we should walk in them.
EPHESIANS 2:10

The Church Is Born

READ LUKE 24:36-53 AND ACTS 1:1-12.

1. The Book of Acts continues Luke's Gospel account and records the events surrounding the birth of the first-century church. How do the narrative accounts of these books overlap?

2. What did Jesus open the disciples' minds to understand at the conclusion of Lukc?

3. What did Jesus say should be proclaimed and to whom? Where would it begin?

4. What did Jesus say was the Father's promise, according to Acts 1:4-5? fWhen was it fulfilled (see Acts 2)?

5. How did God empower His people to carry out His mission?

6. Verse 8 serves as an outline for the Book of Acts. What did Jesus want His disciples to do with this power?

7. What question did the angels ask those who were looking into the clouds?

8. What truth did these messengers bring?

9. Why did the disciples travel to Jerusalem?

10. What followed their obedience (see Acts 2)?

MEDITATE ON THE FOLLOWING VERSE.

You will receive power when the Holy Spirit has come
upon you, and you will be my witnesses in Jerusalem and
in all Judea and Samaria, and to the end of the earth.
ACTS 1:8

Predestined to the Praise of His Glory

READ EPHESIANS 1:3-14.

1. What has God done for those in Christ (see vv. 3-6)? Why?

2. Whom should we praise? What word did Paul use to express his affections for Christ?

3. What do we have in Christ? According to what (see v. 7)?

4. What was God's purpose in making His will known?

5. What have we obtained? According to what? Why (see v. 11)?

6. Whom did we receive as a seal, guaranteeing our inheritance?

Paul's Testimony Before Agrippa

READ ACTS 26.

1. Who was Paul's audience (see Acts 25)?

2. In Acts 26 how did Paul describe himself before his conversion?

3. Before his conversion what happened to Paul when he lived in active opposition to Christ?

4. For what purpose did Christ reveal himself to Paul?

5. How was Paul obedient to that purpose?

6. What was Paul's message?

7. How did the Jews receive this message?

8. Who helped Paul in his testimony?

9. What did Festus say about Paul's testimony?

10. Was Paul saved in order to take his blessings and keep them to himself or to share them with others?

11. What was Agrippa's final question to Paul? How did Paul respond?

MEDITATE ON THE FOLLOWING VERSES.

Before all this they will lay their hands on you and persecute you, delivering you up to the synagogues and prisons, and you will be brought before kings and governors for my name's sake. This will be your opportunity to bear witness. Settle it therefore in your minds not to meditate beforehand how to answer, for I will give you a mouth and wisdom, which none of your adversaries will be able to withstand or contradict.
LUKE 21:12-15

Even if you should suffer for righteousness' sake, you will be blessed. Have no fear of them, nor be troubled, but in your hearts honor Christ the Lord as holy, always being prepared to make a defense to anyone who asks you for a reason for the hope that is in you; yet do it with gentleness and respect, having a good conscience, so that, when you are slandered, those who revile your good behavior in Christ may be put to shame.
1 PETER 3:14-16

Power and Persecution

... strengthening the souls of the disciples, encouraging
them to continue in the faith, and saying that through
many tribulations we must enter the kingdom of God.

ACTS 14:22

READ ACTS 5:12-42.

1. Why did the Sadducees have the apostles arrested (see v. 17)?

2. What happened while the apostles were in prison? What were they instructed to say?

3. How did the apostles respond?

4. What did the officers find when they brought the apostles before the courts?

5. Why were the officers afraid of using force with the apostles (see v. 26)?

6. What did the council strictly charge the apostles not to do?

7. How did the apostles respond? What was their message?

> [Jesus] opened their minds to understand the Scriptures, and said to them, "Thus it is written, that the Christ should suffer and on the third day rise from the dead, and that repentance and forgiveness of sins should be proclaimed in his name to all nations, beginning from Jerusalem. You are witnesses of these things. And behold, I am sending the promise of my Father upon you. But stay in the city until you are clothed with power from on high."
> **LUKE 24:45-49**

8. Compare the previous passage with Acts 1:8. What did Jesus promise and for what purpose?

9. How did the council respond to the truth, according to Acts 5:33?

10. What wisdom did Gamaliel offer?

11. In light of this advice, what did the council do with the apostles?

12. How did the apostles respond to this treatment (see v. 41)?

13. As a result, what did they continue doing?

Jesus Washes the Disciples' Feet

[Christ Jesus] emptied himself, by taking the form of a servant, being
born in the likeness of men. And being found in human form, he humbled
himself by becoming obedient to the point of death, even death on a cross.
PHILIPPIANS 2:7-8

READ JOHN 13:1-19.

1. How did Jesus demonstrate His love for His disciples on His last night
   with them?

2. What virtue did it take to disrobe, kneel, and wash others' feet?

3. Why does it seem extraordinary that Jesus would serve this way with
   the full knowledge of what would soon take place?

4. How did Peter respond to Jesus' offer to wash his feet?

5. What spiritual truth and example did Jesus' response communicate?

6. How did Jesus characterize those who follow His example (see v. 17)?

7. Notice that Jesus washed even the feet of Judas. What does that act say about whom we should be willing to serve?

MEDITATE ON THE FOLLOWING VERSE.

Jesus called them to him and said, "You know that the rulers of the Gentiles lord it over them, and their great ones exercise authority over them. It shall not be so among you. But whoever would be great among you must be your servant, and whoever would be first among you must be your slave, even as the Son of Man came not to be served but to serve, and to give his life as a ransom for many."
MATTHEW 20:25-28

Going Deeper

1. How has God blessed you so that you can be a blessing to others?

2. How has God gifted you with spiritual gifts from the Holy Spirit? How will you use those gifts to serve and build up the body of Christ? Be specific.

3. How will you use the testimony of God's grace in your life to guide others toward Christ?

> They have conquered him by the blood of the Lamb and by the word
> of their testimony, for they loved not their lives even unto death.
> **REVELATION 12:11**

4. Where has God placed you to serve? How do you think others would describe your heart for service?

5. God has called us to make disciples. How will you apply what you have learned through this discipleship process to make disciples for Christ?

6. Acts 17 shows us, through Paul's missionary experiences, that God places us at the exact time and place where He wants to use us. How are you living missionally within your community?

7. How will you continue to practice all you have learned through the *Steps* process? Who will keep you accountable?

8. With what attitude will you engage or reengage with the world around you? Is there any obstacle or excuse that would keep you from doing so?

9. The Book of Joshua recounts the Lord's powerful deliverance of the promised land to the Israelites. As they stepped out in faith, He held back the raging waters of the Jordan River so that they could cross to safety. The Israelites picked up stones from the riverbed to remind them of the Lord's faithfulness. As you have stepped out in faith, in what ways has God demonstrated His faithfulness during this particular season of your life?

STEP 12: Having had a spiritual experience as the result of these steps, we try to carry this message to others and to practice these principles in all our affairs.

> Jesus came and said to them, "All authority in heaven and on earth has been given to me. Go therefore and make disciples of all nations, baptizing them in the name of the Father and of the Son and of the Holy Spirit, teaching them to observe all that I have commanded you. And behold, I am with you always, to the end of the age."
> **MATTHEW 28:18-20**

You will receive power when the Holy Spirit has come upon
you; and you will be my witnesses in Jerusalem, and in
all Judea and Samaria, and to the ends of the earth.
ACTS 1:8

They have conquered him by the blood of the Lamb and by the word
of their testimony, for they loved not their lives even unto death.
REVELATION 12:11

You are the light of the world. A city set on a hill cannot be hidden.
Nor do people light a lamp and put it under a basket, but on a
stand, and it gives light to all in the house. In the same way, let
your light shine before others, so that they may see your good
works and give glory to your Father who is in heaven.
MATTHEW 5:14-16

From him and through him and to him are
all things. To him be glory forever. Amen.
ROMANS 11:36

To me, though I am the very least of all the saints, this grace was
given, to preach to the Gentiles the unsearchable riches of Christ,
and to bring to light for everyone what is the plan of the mystery
hidden for ages in God who created all things, so that through
the church the manifold wisdom of God might now be made
known to the rulers and authorities in the heavenly places.
EPHESIANS 3:8-10

REDEEMED TRUTH FROM STEP 12: Before the foundations of the earth, God chose us, the church, to live as messengers of reconciliation to a lost and dying world, bearing witness to His wisdom and power through the gospel of Jesus Christ. It is our joy-filled worship to make much of His name, empowered by the Holy Spirit in bringing a comprehensive gospel demonstrated by our deeds and proclaimed by our words, with the goal of making disciples for Jesus Christ. In this same way, we incarnate Christ, being His hands and feet on the earth.

REDEEMING THE 12 STEPS THROUGH THE GOSPEL

STEP 1: We admitted we were powerless over our addictions and compulsive behaviors—that our lives had become unmanageable.

REDEEMED TRUTH FROM STEP 1: Man, in relationship to his Creator, has fallen from a place of dignity, humility, and dependence to a state of depravity, pride, and rebellion. This has led to unfathomable suffering. Any attempts on our own to redeem ourselves are futile, only increasing the problem of independence and self-sufficiency. Any perceived success leads only to empty vanity. Apart from Christ, we are powerless to overcome sin, and our attempts to control it only increase our chaos.

STEP 2: We came to believe that a power greater than ourselves could restore us to sanity.

REDEEMED TRUTH FROM STEP 2: God lovingly intervened into our chaos and provided a remedy for the insanity of sin and the way back into fellowship with Him. We believe that by grace through faith in Jesus Christ, we can be redeemed.

STEP 3: We made a decision to turn our will and our lives over to the care of God, as you understand Him.

REDEEMED TRUTH FROM STEP 3: Through the Holy Spirit's illumination of our desperate and helpless condition before God and from the hope that comes through the gospel of Jesus Christ, we step out in faith and repent as an act of worship and obedience, surrendering our will and entrusting our lives to Christ's care and control. We are reborn spiritually and rescued from the domain of darkness and brought into the kingdom of light, where we now live as a part of Christ's ever-advancing kingdom.

STEP 4: We made a searching and fearless moral assessment of ourselves.

REDEEMED TRUTH FROM STEP 4: As children of God armed with the Holy Spirit and standing firm in the gospel, we engage in the spiritual battle over the reign and rule of our hearts. God set us apart for holiness, and we look to put to death the areas of our lives that keep us from reflecting Jesus Christ to a dark and dying world. We first examine the fruit in our lives (or moral symptoms). As we move through the assessment process, we will uncover the roots of any ungodly fruit (pride and idolatry) that drive our ungodly thoughts, actions, and emotions.

STEP 5: We admitted before God, ourselves, and another human being the exact nature of our wrongs.

REDEEMED TRUTH FROM STEP 5: Under the covering of God's grace, we step out in faith, leaving behind our old, self-protective ways of covering sin and hiding from God. We prayerfully come into the light, confessing our sins before God and to one another so that we may be healed.

STEP 6: We are entirely ready to have God remove all these defects of character.

STEP 7: We humbly asked Him to remove our shortcomings.

REDEEMED TRUTH FROM STEPS 6 & 7: In attempting to live independent of God, we have developed dysfunctional (sinful) patterns of coping. After careful examination we have begun to see the demonic roots of our slavery to these sinful patterns. We desire freedom. We renounce our former ways; offer ourselves to God; and, under the waterfall of His grace, ask Him to deliver and heal us by the authority of Christ and the power of the Holy Spirit. We also pray for blessing and the empowerment of the Holy Spirit to live life according to His kingdom purposes.

STEP 8: We made a list of all persons we had harmed and became willing to make amends to them all.

STEP 9: We made direct amends to such people whenever possible, except when to do so would injure them or others.

REDEEMED TRUTH FROM STEPS 8 & 9: Relationships break down because of sin. If there were no sin in the world, relationships would work harmoniously, evidenced by love and unity. Division among God's people provides opportunities to identify sin and purify the body. The gospel of Jesus Christ brings about justice in a way that the law cannot by inwardly reconciling the very heart of injustice to God. As those forgiven by God, we can humbly approach those affected by our sin and make amends. This change of heart brings glory to God by demonstrating the power of the gospel and reflecting His heart in bringing justice through His reconciled people.

ADDITIONAL REDEEMED TRUTH FROM STEPS 8 AND 9: As ambassadors of Christ, we are to be instruments of grace as we confront those who sin against us. We hand our offenses over to God and extend eager forgiveness to those who ask for it. And in this way, fellowship with God and among His people is preserved.

STEP 10: We continued to take personal inventory and, when we were wrong, promptly admitted it.

STEP 11: We sought through prayer and meditation to improve our conscious contact with God, praying only for the knowledge of His will and the power to carry that out.

REDEEMED TRUTH FROM STEPS 10 & 11: We continue in the fear of the Lord, putting to death those things that rob our affections for Christ while persevering in our loving and joyful obedience to Him. We return to the Lord quickly with an attitude of repentance, when out of step with the Spirit, as we're trained in godliness and grow spiritually. Since He is our ultimate treasure, we seek to know Him and fill ourselves with those things that stir our affections for Him. We practice spiritual disciplines so that our hearts, so prone to wander, might stay in rhythm with His.

STEP 12: Having had a spiritual experience as the result of these steps, we try to carry this message to others and to practice these principles in all our affairs.

REDEEMED TRUTH FROM STEP 12: Before the foundations of the earth, God chose us, the church, to live as messengers of reconciliation to a lost and dying world, bearing witness to His wisdom and power through the gospel of Jesus Christ. It is our joy-filled worship to make much of His name, empowered by the Holy Spirit in bringing a comprehensive gospel demonstrated by our deeds and proclaimed by our words, with the goal of making disciples for Jesus Christ. In this same way, we incarnate Christ, being His hands and feet on the earth.

APPENDIX B

THE IDENTITY OF A BELIEVER IN UNION WITH JESUS CHRIST

IDENTITY IN CHRIST

Matthew 5:13	I am the salt of the earth.
Matthew 5:14	I am the light of the world.
John 1:12	I am a child of God.
John 15	I am part of the true vine, a branch of Christ's life.
John 15:15	I am a friend of God.
John 15:16	I am chosen and appointed to bear fruit.
Romans 6:5	I am resurrected to new life.
Romans 6:18	I am a slave to righteousness.
Romans 6:22	I am enslaved to God.
Romans 8:14	I am a son of God.
Romans 8:17	I am a joint heir with Christ, sharing his inheritance.
1 Corinthians 6:19	I am the dwelling place of God.
1 Corinthians 6:19	I am united to the Lord.
1 Corinthians 12:27	I am a member of Christ's body.
1 Corinthians 15:10	I am what I am, by God's grace.
2 Corinthians 5:17	I am a new creation.
2 Corinthians 5:18-19	I am reconciled to God.
Galatians 3:29	I am the seed of Abraham.
Galatians 4:6-7	I am an heir of God since I am a son of God.
Ephesians 1:1	I am a saint.
Ephesians 1:3	I am blessed with every spiritual blessing.
Ephesians 2:10	I am God's workmanship, made to do good works.
Ephesians 2:11	I am a fellow citizen of God's family.
Ephesians 4:1	I am a prisoner of Christ.
Ephesians 4:24	I am righteous and holy.
Philippians 3:20	I am a citizen of heaven.
Colossians 3:3	I am hidden with Christ in God.
Colossians 3:4	I am an expression of the life of Christ.
Colossians 3:12	I am chosen of God, holy and dearly loved.
1 Thessalonians 5:5	I am a child of light and not darkness.
Titus 3:7	I am an heir to eternal life.
Hebrews 3:1	I am a holy partaker of a heavenly calling.
1 Peter 2:5	I am a living stone in God's spiritual house.
1 Peter 2:9	I am a member of a chosen race, a holy nation.

1 Peter 2:9-10	I am a priest.
1 Peter 2:11	I am an alien and a stranger to the world.
1 Peter 5:8	I am an enemy of the Devil.
2 Peter 1:3	I am participating in the divine nature.
1 John 5:18	I am born of God, and the Devil cannot touch me.

IDENTITY APART FROM CHRIST

Genesis 6:5	I am wicked and evil.
Isaiah 59:2	I am separated from God.
Isaiah 64:6	I am filthy and stained.
John 8:34	I am a slave to sin.
Romans 1:18	I am under the wrath of God.
Romans 3:10	I am not good.
Romans 3:23	I am falling short of the glory of God.
Romans 5:26	I am guilty and condemned.
2 Corinthians 4:4	I am blind to the truth.
2 Corinthians 11:3	I am deceived.
Ephesians 2:1	I am dead in my sins.
Ephesians 2:2	I am in bondage to Satan.
Ephesians 4:18	I am hard-hearted.
James 2:10	I am a lawbreaker.
James 4:4	I am an enemy of God.

APPENDIX C

GOD'S PROMISES TO A BELIEVER

Matthew 6:25-30	God will provide for your needs.
Matthew 11:28-30	Rest in Christ.
Matthew 21:22	Ask in His name, and you will receive.
Matthew 24:9-14	Persecution is coming.
Matthew 26:29	He is waiting to eat with you.
Matthew 28:20	He is with us always, to the end of age.
Mark 16:16	Whoever believes and is baptized will be saved.
Luke 12:27-34	He knows what you need; seek His kingdom, and what you need will be provided.
John 14:1-4	Jesus is preparing a place for you.
John 14:13-14	Ask in Jesus' name, and He will do it so that the Father can be glorified in the Son.
John 14:27	He gives us His peace.

John 15:7-8	If you remain in Him, ask whatever you want.
John 15:5	If you remain in Christ, you will produce fruit.
John 16:13-15	The Holy Spirit will guide you into all truth.
John 16:23-24	Ask the Father in Jesus' name, and it will be given so that your joy may be full.
Acts 1:8	You will receive power when the Holy Spirit comes.
Acts 1:38-39	The promise is for you, the believer.
Romans 6:14	Sin will not rule over you.
Romans 8:27	The Holy Spirit intercedes for the saints according to the will of God.
Romans 8:34	Jesus is at the right hand of the Father interceding for you.
Romans 8:39	Nothing will have the power to separate you from the love of God in Jesus Christ.
1 Corinthians 1:8	He will strengthen you till the end.
1 Corinthians 2:13	The Holy Spirit will teach you.
1 Corinthians 2:16	You have been given the mind of Christ.
1 Corinthians 10:13	God will not allow you to be tempted beyond what you are able, and He will provide a way out.
1 Corinthians 15:52-57	You will be raised into an incorruptible immortal body at the resurrection of the dead.
2 Corinthians 3:18	You are being transformed into the image of Christ.
Philipians 1:6	He who started a good work in you will complete it.
Philipians 3:21-22	He will transform the body of our humble condition into the likeness of His glorious body.
Philipians 4:7	The peace of God will guard your heart and mind in Jesus Christ.
1 Thessalonians 5:24	He who calls you is faithful, who will also do it.
2 Thessalonians 3:3	The lord is faithful and will strengthen and guard you from the Evil One.
Titus 3: 6-7	He has abundantly poured out His Spirit on us through Jesus, and we are heirs to the hope of eternal life.
Hebrews 7:25	He is able to save all who come to Him, and He always intercedes for them.
Hebrews 8:8-12	God will never again remember your sins.
Hebews 10:16-17	In the new covenant God will never again remember your sins or your lawless acts.
Hebrews 13:5	God will never leave or forsake you.
1 Peter 1:3-5	Inheritance is imperishable, undefiled, uncorrupted, unfading, kept in heaven for you.
1 Peter 2:10	You are now a part of God's people.
Revelation 21:1-7	God will dwell with us and wipe away every tear, and death will no longer exist.

THE INSANITY CYCLE OF SIN

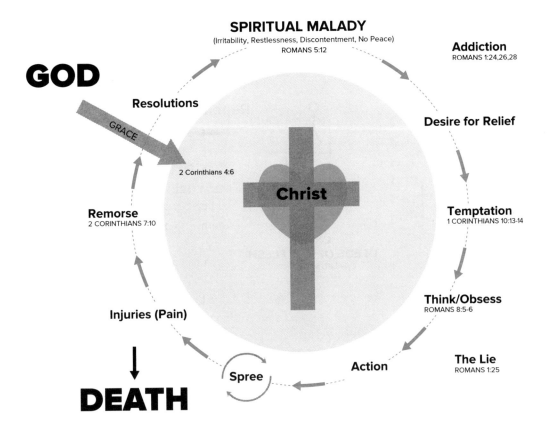

THE THREE CIRCLES: A GOD-CENTERED LIFE

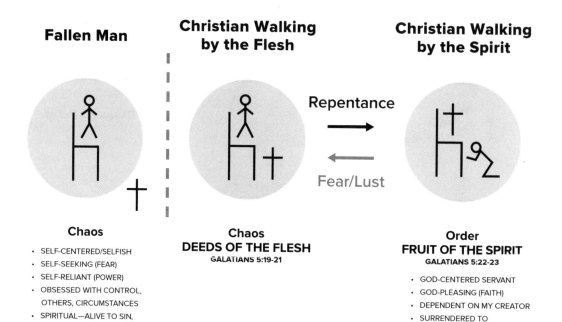

Fallen Man

Christian Walking by the Flesh

Christian Walking by the Spirit

Repentance

Fear/Lust

Chaos

- SELF-CENTERED/SELFISH
- SELF-SEEKING (FEAR)
- SELF-RELIANT (POWER)
- OBSESSED WITH CONTROL, OTHERS, CIRCUMSTANCES
- SPIRITUAL—ALIVE TO SIN, DEAD TO GOD

Chaos
DEEDS OF THE FLESH
GALATIANS 5:19-21

Order
FRUIT OF THE SPIRIT
GALATIANS 5:22-23

- GOD-CENTERED SERVANT
- GOD-PLEASING (FAITH)
- DEPENDENT ON MY CREATOR
- SURRENDERED TO GOD'S SOVEREIGNTY

Adapted from Campus Crusade for Christ